The LASER Fund

How to Diversify and Create the Foundation
for a Tax-Free Retirement

Seotion II
[The Right-Brain Approach]

Dougla Andrew

Emron Andrew

Aaron Andrew

UPDATED EDITION
3DimensionalWealth.com

Also by Douglas Andrew, Emron Andrew, Aaron Andrew
Millionaire by Thirty

Also by Douglas Andrew

Best-Sellers

Missed Fortune
Missed Fortune 101
The Last Chance Millionaire

Entitlement Abolition
Learning Curves
Secrets to a Tax-Free Retirement
Baby Boomer Blunders
Create Your Own Economic Stimulus
How to Have LASER Focus

Original edition published 2018
Updated edition published 2022
By 3 Dimensional Wealth
Salt Lake City, UT U.S.A.
Printed in U.S.A.

ISBN: 978-0-9740087-4-5

The LASER Fund and The IUL LASER Fund are proprietary terms used by the authors of this book as a way to describe a properly structured, maximum-funded Indexed Universal Life (IUL) policy. With any mention of LASER Funds, IUL LASER Funds, properly structured, maximum-funded IUL policies, or related financial vehicle terms throughout this book, let it be noted that any life insurance policy is not an investment and, accordingly, should not be purchased as an investment.

Where appropriate, authentic examples of clients' policies have been incorporated, with names changed to safeguard privacy.

The materials in this book represent the opinions of the authors and may not be applicable to all situations. Due to the frequency of changing laws and regulations, some aspects of this work may be out of date, even upon first publication. Accordingly, the authors and publisher assume no responsibility for actions taken by readers based upon the advice offered in this book. You should use caution in applying the material contained in this book to your specific situation and should seek competent advice from a qualified professional or IUL specialist. Please provide your comments directly to the authors.

Acknowledgements

We would like to thank the many clients who have shared their journey toward greater abundance with us over the past decades.

We have been privileged to support them in utilizing The IUL LASER Fund, that has helped them take advantage of greater liquidity, safety, rates of return, and tax advantages. We have also been fortunate to share many aspects of developing true abundance—a holistic approach to life and legacy that encompasses all 3 Dimensions of Authentic Wealth, as we highlight here in Section II, Chapter 1.

We are blessed to be associated with outstanding professionals who also work to deliver optimal strategies to their clients. We'd like to specifically thank the following financial professionals for their contributions to Section II: Greg Duckwitz; Brian Gibbs; Karl Nelson; Bill Newport; Ed Sanderson; Scott Reynolds; and Bill Zimmerman.

In this section of the book, we share many of their experiences here (with names and details changed to protect privacy). We applaud them for working together to pursue brighter futures, for carrying on in the face of losses, and for choosing paths that benefit those they care about—for generations to come.

Table of Contents

1 Truly Abundant Living 1

2 The LASER Fund for ... Death Benefit 15

3 The LASER Fund for ... Retirement Planning..................... 23

4 The LASER Fund for ... Working Capital 29

5 The LASER Fund for ... School, Family, and Life 35

6 The LASER Fund for ... Lump Sums 41

7 The LASER Fund for ... Business Planning 47

8 The LASER Fund for ... Life's Emergencies 55

9 The LASER Fund for ... Estate Planning 61

10 The LASER Fund for ... Real Estate 67

11 The LASER Fund for ... Strategic Rollouts 75

12 The LASER Fund for ... Tax Reduction 81

[For the Left-Brain Approach – Flip to Section I]

Truly Abundant Living

The Olympics. Citizens around the globe gather around their televisions, mobile devices, and radios to witness the epic two-week-long competition. They cheer on their nation's top contenders, inspired by stories of strength, tenacity, and perseverance.

What's fascinating—and enlightening—is to understand that those stellar athletes don't reach that exclusive level of performance solely by practicing skills required for their sport. The sprinters don't just race around the track. The slalom skiers don't just hit the slopes. The swimmers don't just do laps. No, world-class athletes follow well-balanced regimens.

They fuel up on foods and nutritionals tailored to their specific needs. They cross-train and strength-train to maximize their body's potential. They practice mental wellness and glean from sports psychology. They recover through stretching, hydration, and sleep. They incorporate all dimensions of athletic excellence, because sports science has proven that a myopic approach doesn't yield the best outcomes. It takes a holistic strategy to achieve superior results.

MORE THAN JUST MONEY

Our lives are similar. For a truly abundant life, it takes more than just financial success. But this is a revolutionary thought for some. There have been entire empires built on the quest for money and riches, entire family dynasties dedicated to the almighty dollar. In Doug's book, *Entitlement Abolition*, he shares the story of the Vanderbilts, a wealthy American family whose fortunes began with patriarch Cornelius Vanderbilt.

Throughout the nineteenth century, Cornelius rose from a lowly farmer and ferryman to a steamboat captain and eventually the owner of steamship and railroad companies. By the time he died at age 82, he had amassed the highest individual fortune in America at the time—more than $100 million—beating out the size of the US Treasury.

Cornelius was famously not a philanthropist, with only two notable acts of charity: a donation during the Civil War to aid the North, and a $1 million donation to found Vanderbilt University, offered just three years before his death. In fact, he was known for being so stingy that he was called out by contemporary Mark Twain, who urged him to contribute to society with a scathing open letter that included lines such as, "You observe that I haven't said anything about your soul, Vanderbilt. It is because I have evidence that you haven't any."

Cornelius' poor reputation for charitable giving continued into future generations, with just a few descendants proving an exception to the rule, including the third generation's William K. Vanderbilt, who gave to Vanderbilt University, Columbia University, and housing for the poor in Manhattan, and the fourth generation's Gertrude Vanderbilt Whitney, who co-founded the Whitney Museum of American Art in New York City.

As for the Vanderbilts' financial legacy, Cornelius' son William "Billy" Vanderbilt took the reins and doubled the family fortune to over $200 million, but then things turned. Within thirty years of the Commodore's death, no member of the Vanderbilt family was among the richest in America. The third generations' lavish spending deteriorated the family wealth, and by the fourth generation, the family fortune was considered squandered.

Contrast the Vanderbilts' approach to abundance with the Rothschilds', whose rise to prominence began during the mid-eighteenth century, with Mayer Amschel Rothschild. Now, as we share highlights of the Rothschild family, let us note that while we may not agree with everything the Rothschilds have done or supported, their story provides a valuable example of wealth accumulation and preservation throughout generations.

It all started with Mayer Amschel, who launched his career dealing in coins and went on to found a banking dynasty, which his five sons helped expand across Europe. As their fortune grew, the Rothschilds established a system for perpetuating family wealth and values.

Rather than merely dumping family wealth on next generations to spend at will, if family members wanted to borrow money for business ventures or other needs, they were required to repay those loans back to the family bank. Family members were also required to take part in annual family gatherings where they would share their knowledge and reaffirm their values. Their approach to family and business is summarized in their motto: *Concordia, Integritas, Industria,* Latin for unity, integrity, and hard work. Now, over 200 years since Mayer Amschel launched his family business, the Rothschild financial legacy continues, with an estimated family net worth in the hundreds of billions of dollars.

The Rothschilds also placed a high priority on philanthropy. From the early 1800s until today, generations of Rothschilds have established and maintained foundations and efforts to provide support for everything from health care and medical research to the arts, cultural heritage, housing, social welfare, and human rights.

These high-profile family comparisons illustrate an important point. Passing along what we call "Authentic Wealth" is about much more than money. For a rewarding—and enduring—journey, you need to focus on accumulating more than a high net worth. You need to develop a high net *life,* and pass along the ability to perpetuate that abundant life to your posterity.

3 DIMENSIONS OF AUTHENTIC WEALTH

Through our work with thousands of clients, and through our collaboration with leading national think tanks and professional organizations, we've gleaned the critical essentials of abundant living. We've distilled these aspects of the "swing" into a practical system. At the core of this system are what we call the 3 Dimensions of Authentic Wealth:

- **The Financial Dimension** – This dimension includes anything to do with your money: cash, real estate, savings, CDs, money market accounts, stocks, bonds, traditional retirement plans, non-traditional accounts for retirement, IUL LASER Funds, etc. (as a note, we use IUL LASER Funds and LASER Funds interchangeably throughout this book to represent a properly structured, maximum-funded Indexed Universal Life policy).

- **The Foundational Dimension** – This dimension incorporates your relationships and values, including: family, friends, health, well-being, spirituality, talents, heritage, character, and charitable giving.

- **The Intellectual Dimension** – This dimension is comprised of the wisdom you gain through life—a combination of knowledge and experience—such as: formal education, effective systems and methods, valuable traditions, business and personal alliances, powerful ideas, and critical skills.

For a life of lasting abundance, it's essential to develop not just one, not two, but all 3 Dimensions of Authentic Wealth. This holistic approach can help ensure that you are maintaining a balance, one that can foster sustained growth in every aspect.

We realize it's one thing to read about these 3 Dimensions on paper, but how do you take them from theory to practical application? How exactly do you cultivate these dimensions in real life?

For the Financial Dimension, Section I of this book is your guide. You can start with a strong foundation, The IUL LASER Fund, to maximize your serious money, money you want to set aside for growth. With about 20% to 40% of your income or net worth in The IUL LASER Fund, the rest of your money should be put to work in complementary vehicles that can provide as much liquidity, safety, predictable rates of return, and tax advantages as possible.

Now when it comes to the Foundational and Intellectual Dimensions, our Abundant Living Coaches offer a comprehensive program to help people incorporate Habits of Abundance. We'll highlight a few of those key practices here in this chapter:

- Establish Equal Opportunity vs. Equal Distribution
- Design Your KASH Blueprint
- Establish Your Legacy Bank

FISH, GOLF & LINCOLN

Before we delve into those practices, we want to pause and take a look at how we talk about perpetuating generational wealth. We often frame it with the adage, "Give a man a fish, and you feed him for a day. Teach a man to fish, and you feed him for a lifetime." In *Entitlement Abolition,* Doug explores this concept in-depth, pointing out that it's common for well-intended parents—particularly those of financial means—to "dump" the fish in their children's laps, rather than teaching them how to fish. Parents give their children free access to money, cars, travel, and affluent lifestyles in an effort to help them, but this approach can actually achieve the opposite. It stunts children's development, and like the Vanderbilts, can eventually lead to squandered wealth—and lives.

Here's another way to look at the issue: if you were going to be playing in a golf tournament and had the choice of using a professional golfer's swing—or you could use his golf clubs—which would you prefer? We would choose his swing. This way, no matter which course you were playing or which set of clubs you happened to be using, you'd have the skills necessary to succeed.

The same holds true in life. If you learn the proper swing—proven skills and strategies—even when you encounter setbacks or downfalls, you have the ability to rebuild and succeed. And, you are able to pass along the swing to every child and grandchild, so they can move forward and do the same (which isn't always the case with the clubs—there are only so many to go around, and they can get bent).

Another way to stop the entitlement cycle is exemplified in an anecdote we share in our Habits of Abundance program. The perspective comes from a letter that President Abraham Lincoln wrote to his step-brother, John Daniel Johnston. In the letter, Lincoln explains why he will not comply with his step-brother's request to give him $80. Lincoln explains that previous handouts haven't been long-term solutions, and he fears that giving his step-brother yet another $80 will only perpetuate the problem. (In context, this would be equivalent to about seven to ten months' worth of income, as farm laborers were paid $8 to $12 a month in 1850, according to the National Bureau of Economic Research.)

He offers an honest critique, saying, "I doubt whether, since I saw you, you have done a good whole day's work in any one day.... This habit of uselessly wasting time is the whole difficulty; it is vastly important to you, and still more so to your children, that you should break the habit."

He proposes that Johnston go to work "tooth and nail," and whatever sum he earns over the next few months, Lincoln will match. He explains the result will be invaluable: "Now, if you will do this, you will be soon out of debt, and, what is better, you will have a habit that will keep you from getting in debt again.... If you will but follow my advice, you will find it worth more than eighty times eighty dollars to you."

Lincoln understood the value of putting some skin in the game. He knew the only way for his brother to break free from the entitlement trap would be to get in motion and resolve his own challenges. Lincoln had no problem giving a hand up—he just knew it would be better than giving a handout.

As you look at your own family and consider the value of teaching them how to fish or coaching them on the pro swing, it's important to keep in mind that each child is unique. Think about it: if you have one child in elementary school and another in high school, do you teach and discipline them the exact same way? No, because we know an eight-year-old and sixteen-year-old are at completely different levels of experience, comprehension, skills, and development.

Beyond developmental differences, children come with their own "factory-installed" personalities, talents, strengths, weaknesses, temperaments, and gifts. As Dr. Edward Hallowell, best-selling author, has said, it's parents' role to "unwrap their gifts." As you do, you come to the realization that what works for one child may absolutely fail with another, and that it often takes individual strategies to motivate each child and raise them effectively.

As your children enter adulthood and pursue goals in education, career, family, home ownership, and more, they are likely going to handle life uniquely, with different levels of momentum, commitment, aptitude, etc.

So whether it's the advice and wisdom you impart, or the financial backup you provide, realistically, you want to approach each child differently.

Say, for example, your teenager asks to borrow the snowmobile for a day of fun with his friends. He takes a steep hill too fast and rolls the vehicle. In a world where you're teaching accountability, rather than saying, "No problem Jon, I'll pay for the repairs," you involve Jon in resolving the situation. If Jon has an after–school job, you set up a realistic timeline for him to repay you for the repairs. Or if Jon doesn't have a job but he's adept at woodworking, he contracts with you to use his skills and time to repair the backyard fence, which you agree will offset the cost of repairs.

Throughout this chapter, we'll explore how families can honor individual differences while reinforcing accountability and responsibility, and pro–viding equal opportunities.

EQUAL OPPORTUNITY VS. EQUAL DISTRIBUTION

When considering how you transfer wealth to your children, convention–al advice often calls for equal distribution. If you have five children, when you pass on, your estate value should be divided into five equal parts so every child gets her or his share. That's fair, right? And fair is always good ... right?

Over the decades, we have reviewed hundreds of trusts. The vast majority of them are designed to administer equal distribution. The challenge is, we have seen that approach fail in achieving optimal results time and again. In all kinds of situations—from moderate estates to those of high net worth with a labyrinth of assets—there is often squabbling if not outright infighting over whether estate shares are equal. Even after the distribu–tion, some beneficiaries may maximize their share while others squander theirs, which can lead to further discontent. It reminds us of the adage, "United we stand, divided we fall." Too many families fall apart when the fish is divided equally then dumped into the next generation's laps.

Instead, we champion a different approach to wealth transfer: equal opportunity. It's a strategy based on principles of ownership and ac–countability, of living in a proactive zone of empowerment with predict–able results, rather than in the reactive zone of entitlement, with hope and despair. It's about passing on the swing (how to thrive in all Three

Dimensions of Authentic Wealth), rather than the clubs (handing over the financial assets).

With an equal opportunity approach, your financial assets are placed into what we call an Equal Opportunity Trust, a revocable living trust with rules of governance for equal opportunity, rather than equal distribution. This document includes clear parameters guiding how your heirs can access the assets you leave behind. Your trust may specify that some withdrawals should be taken as loans, with accompanying repayment requirements. Other withdrawals may be granted without repayment. However you organize your trust, just keep in mind the most critical strategy: weaving equal opportunity—and equal responsibility—throughout the guidelines. This will help alleviate any ambiguity or disputes when no longer around to referee.

This equal opportunity approach is so powerful, it can positively impact your family BEFORE you pass on, as well. It all starts with creating a plan that outlines the distribution of your cash ... and KASH.

DESIGN YOUR KASH BLUEPRINT

As you may guess, when we talk about cash, we're talking literally about the money that fuels your Financial Dimension, which can ignite all types of worthwhile pursuits: education, business ventures, charitable giving, and more. KASH, on the other hand, is a term we've coined to encompass Knowledge, Attitudes, Skills, and Habits. If nurtured, this type of KASH can be just as valuable, if not more. It can be a perpetual force, powering your life and that of future generations to Intellectual and Foundational abundance. It's the knowledge of how to fish, the pro's swing, the Lincoln letter to posterity to get some skin in the game. Just like a financial trust ensures your money transfers smoothly after you pass away, you can create a plan for the transfer and flow of your family's 3 Dimensions of Authentic Wealth while you're living: a KASH Blueprint.

There are two facets of your KASH Blueprint:

1. KASH Values & Vision
2. KASH Rules of Governance

Your KASH Values & Vision is much like the U.S. Declaration of Independence. It's a written statement that outlines your beliefs, the principles you hold dear, the guiding tenets that will mark the path for your family to follow as they journey through life. It can be a handful of words, or it can be a several-page document—whatever works best for you.

Your KASH Rules of Governance are like the U.S. Constitution. The principles establish the "laws," or rules that spell out how your family accesses your Financial Dimension. It should be thorough, outlining strategies for every practical financial aspect of life, such as:

- Education
- Business ventures/loans
- Personal loans
- Supplemental income
- Weddings
- Personal residence
- Health/medical costs
- Emergency needs
- Family Retreats with a Purpose
- Charitable distributions
- Religious or humanitarian missions

For example, let's look at education. We offer a somewhat contrarian view when we say: don't pay for college. At least not entirely. Share the cost of higher education in some way with your children. Whether that's through low-interest loans they repay you after graduating, or having children provide half of the costs, while you match the other half—however you arrange it, do not give away that opportunity for your children to be invested in their own education. The ownership, accountability, and responsibility they apply to their education will inspire them to make the most of the experience.

The same holds true with money your children may request for business ventures, down payments on homes, cars, and more. Rather than forking over the money, hand them a "pitchfork" and have them start bailing hay—in other words, have them join in achieving that goal. That can be in trading actual work, time, and skills for money that you invest. Or it can be in arranging a loan with nominal interest they'll repay over a specific period of time.

This may seem a little "over-the-top" to put such things in writing, to establish clear governing principles and adhere to them. But there's nothing over-the-top about teaching our children the value of responsibility and accountability, about teaching them how to fish, about giving them a hand up rather than a handout.

What's more, by spelling everything out in your KASH Blueprint, you're effectively helping your family avoid the infighting, jealousy and even total destruction of relationships that too-often arise over family wealth. By giving everyone equal opportunity to access money, there can be no squabbles when Older Sister borrows money for a business venture and repays it on time. If Younger Brother needs money for his daughter's wedding, then he has equal opportunity to borrow and repay the loan. The guidelines are in place. Accountability is required. And family unity is preserved.

ESTABLISH YOUR LEGACY BANK

The best way to capture and preserve all of these assets and guiding principles is by establishing a family Legacy Bank. This is not a literal bank, but a conceptual bank, one in which the entire family can participate. A Legacy Bank is essentially a repository for the Foundational and Intellectual Dimensions, as well as rules of governance for your financial assets. It's a virtual exchange place for your family, where everyone from grandparents and parents to children and grandchildren can:

- "Deposit" their KASH (Knowledge, Attitudes, Skills and Habits)
- Make "withdrawals," borrowing from others' experiences to turn long learning curves into "power curves" and build on generational momentum
- Maintain your KASH Blueprint—with any updates as necessary over the years

While the ins and outs of maintaining a Legacy Bank are explored in-depth in Doug's book, *Entitlement Abolition*, here's a snapshot of how it can work. As the Andrew family, we maintain our Legacy Bank with:

- KASH Values & Vision Statement
- KASH Rules of Governance
- I Remember When Stories
- 3 Dimensional Wealth Tools, including The Better Life Circle and The Negative Experience Transformer
- Family Retreats with a Purpose
- Grandpa's Camp

To illustrate, let's take a look at one of these strategies—I Remember When stories. Once or twice a year at our family gatherings, we invite the entire family (from grandparents to grandchildren ages 4 and up) to share at least one I Remember When story. These are personal stories we bring typed out (750 words or less) and on a thumb drive, to add to our Legacy Bank "library."

The stories can be meaningful, memorable, funny, or even embarrassing (like the time Emron was doing tricks on the handrail, waiting in line at Disneyland—and face-planted into the petunias). They can capture our own love stories (each of us has shared the story of how we met our spouse, and what we value in them). They can teach the value of hard work, like Doug's father's stories of chopping wood and gathering kindling as a young boy to heat his family's home in the wood-burning stove. And they can inspire entrepreneurialism, like Doug's story shared here in Section I, Chapter 5, how the foreclosure on his home led to him becoming passionate about the safety of The IUL LASER Fund.

By sharing these stories on a regular basis, we not only have a system that archives family experiences, but we also grow closer. Grandpa Doug's story of nearly killing himself while installing a zip line at the cabin—thinking he didn't really need the handle bars—brings rounds of laughter, while Grandma Sharee's courage in overcoming severe health challenges uplifts us all.

By leveraging strategies like I Remember When stories, you're setting in motion repeatable processes that can ensure your family preserves critical lessons and insights. You're making it valuable—and fun—to be a part of the tribe that you're creating with your family. Each member feels connected to something larger, something to draw from and contribute to, something important and rewarding.

A SPRINGBOARD FOR THE FINANCIAL DIMENSION

As you focus on all 3 Dimensions of Authentic Wealth, you and your family will be able to enjoy a well-rounded journey toward abundance. You'll capitalize on the Foundational and Intellectual assets. And perhaps most important, this comprehensive approach to Authentic Wealth will be a springboard for maximizing your Financial Dimension.

From this holistic viewpoint, we'll now shift focus to the core message of Section II—multifaceted uses for The IUL LASER Fund. As you move from chapter to chapter, you will see how many ways The IUL LASER Fund can become a "generator" for your future.

We use the term generator rather than battery, because while both provide power, one is more advantageous than the other. Think about it: a battery is limited. If it's your car battery, it may help keep your vehicle going for a while, but after about three to five years, you'll need to replace it. If it's a phone battery, it may not even make it until the end of the day before you have to recharge it.

A generator, on the other hand, can provide power for a much longer span of time and for much greater needs. It simply requires fuel (typically some type of gas or solar energy), and you can use a generator's power for all kinds of things, from providing electricity for big machinery, all the way up to an entire movie set or hospital.

Too often, conventional financial strategies tell you to approach your future by "charging up your retirement battery" just enough to hope that you'll have funds that last as long as you do. But why settle for a limited supply? Why not benefit from a generator that can last, the kind that is charged up with safer, predictable voltage—an IUL LASER Fund that can provide access to income-tax-free money now, and a death benefit for tomorrow? What's more, that death benefit transfers income-tax-free to your heirs, who can in turn place the money into another IUL LASER Fund, providing ongoing, perpetual power for the next generation.

Before you turn the pages, take a moment to score yourself on the complete 3 Dimensional Wealth Scorecard in Figure 1.1. The 3 Dimensional Wealth Scorecard helps you identify where you are currently (and where you want to go). It provides an at-a-glance look at your progress in the Financial Dimension (the top half is the LASER Scorecard from Section I, Chapter 4), and aspects of the Intellectual and Foundational Dimensions. Rank yourself on a scale of 1 – 10, with 10 being superior.

FIGURE 1.1

3 Dimensional Wealth Scorecard

Key Principle	1	2	3	4	5	6	7	8	9	10	Present/ Future
Objective ⇨	Poor ⇨		Fair ⇨		Good ⇨		Better ⇨		Best ⇨		
Liquidity Ability to Access Your Money	Your assets are mostly tied up and cannot be converted quickly to cash for emergencies		You can access your money but could incur penalties or suffer a loss due to markets		You can access your money, but not without incurring cost (by tax or other penalties)		You have predictable cash flow income but have limited access to lump sums, if needed		You have tremendous liquidity and can access your money electronically within hours or a few days		/
Safety of Principal	You're susceptible to market volatility, and the potential for loss is extremely high		Some of your money is in institutions that do not have strong safety ratings		You diversify by offsetting high-risk vehicles with some low-risk vehicles		Your money is in a safe vehicle, but the tradeoff is very low rates of return		Your vehicle has very low risk. Your money is protected from market volatility		/
Rate of Return	Any returns are usually negated by downturns in the market—very little net growth		0%-2% rates of return (pathetically low), while inflation outpaces gains and erodes principal		2%-4% rates of return, and you're set up on a 4% payout to avoid outliving your money		5%-12% average returns, but returns are taxable when you withdraw your money		5-10% historic average returns; tax-free during accumulation and distribution phases; hedging against inflation		/
Tax-Advantaged On the Seed or the Harvest?	Savings and investments are taxed-as-earned (on the seed AND harvest)		Traditional IRAs/401(k)s (tax-deferred accounts); seed money not taxed; pay tax on harvest		Roth IRAs and 401(k)s; pay tax on the seed but a tax-free harvest; IRS limitations/rules		Tax-free accumulation; access and transfer of money with greater flexibility and benefits		Tax advantages on contribution, accumulation, distribution, and transfer phases		/
KASH Generator (vs. a Battery Approach)	You are just hoping to survive and not outlive your money; expenses exceed your income		You're not saving enough to be prepared for retirement; you're always striving to be secure		Your financial battery is getting charged, but taxes and inflation may cause it to die		You have sufficient financial resources; not capturing Knowledge, Attitudes, Skills, Habits		Generating tax-free cash flow in a perpetual fund; transferring cash and KASH as "Generational Wealth"		/
Abundance (vs. a Scarcity Mindset)	You feel resentful and intimidated by others' advantages and often envy their success		You feel guilty about having greater success than others who are close to you		You love to collaborate and share with others, believing that "together we're better"		You have a drive to create greater success so that you can give back to society		You are always making your future bigger than your past by contributing time, talents, and money		/
3 Dimensions (vs. 1 Dimension)	You live in a "mindless reaction state," always putting out fires, trying to fix your problems		Having money, things, or gratification is your primary focus; health and relationships are lacking		Being financially secure is your primary focus, but purpose and values are also important		Authentic Wealth (values and purpose) matters more than money or things		You have extreme clarity, balance, and confidence in life, focused on what matters most		/
Responsibility & Accountability	You often blame others for why you can or can't / did or didn't accomplish something		You justify why you can or can't / did or didn't accomplish something, making excuses		People can count on you to be responsible, but you apologize a lot for not being up to par		You assume total responsibility for yourself and are accountable to others		You always respond with all your ability; are self-reliant and dependable; honor your commitments		/
Equal Opportunity (vs. Equal Distribution)	You do not have any clear guidelines about how to assist those you care about		You find yourself rescuing your children with handouts, greasing squeaky wheels		You have specific rules of "equal distribution" w/assistance to those you care about		You don't want to spoil those you care about, but you probably give (or pay for) too much		You provide equal opportunities for those you care about and require some "skin in the game"		/
Values and Vision Family Creed / Ethical Will	You do not have a written family Values & Vision statement, theme, or document		You have a family motto or theme, but no clear statement of values for what you stand for		You have a family mission statement that family members helped formulate and tweak		You have a family creed that all family members understand and strive to live by		You have a KASH Values & Vision document that will govern how your posterity operates your Legacy Bank		/

If your current score ranges in the 30s – 60s, take heart. That's actually where most people start—and it's been our passion to help thousands of people elevate their scores as quickly as possible (some raising their scores to the 90s within just a year).

Keep your abundant living goals in mind, and if you find you would like a deeper dive into these principles, you may find Doug's book *Entitlement Abolition* helpful, as well as the Entitlement Abolition Kit, a comprehensive program that guides families through 4 modules of abundant living. (www.entitlementabolition.com)

Now prepare to turn the pages, and explore the possibilities for those who harness the power of The IUL LASER Fund in several areas of life.

2
Death Benefit

Karl Nelson (his real name) was an aeronautics engineer, married to the love of his life, and together they were raising their growing family. In their early 40s, he and his wife wanted to initiate financial strategies that could provide the safety of a secure future retirement.

Karl discovered The IUL LASER Fund, and as a technical, analytical person, he investigated the strategies thoroughly. Drawn to the reassurance of a death benefit, the liquidity in case of emergency, and the opportunity for tax-free retirement income, he and his wife opened IUL LASER Fund policies.

Work and family life continued to clip along, until suddenly, everything came to an unexpected halt. Karl's wife was diagnosed with cancer. The family, now with seven children, drew close as she bravely battled the disease. Ultimately, however, she lost the fight, and as Karl bid farewell to his best friend, he looked at his seven children—the youngest two under age 5. He could not bear the thought of them losing their mother and being turned over to day care, so he made a brave decision. He took leave from his career and stayed home to be there for his young ones until they were old enough to enter elementary school.

He was able to do so because of his wife's IUL LASER Fund policy. They had put the policy in place with retirement income in mind, never dreaming it would provide a valuable death benefit sooner than later. That income-tax-free death benefit allowed Karl the financial security to quit his job and care for his children full-time for two years.

Karl's life had been so dramatically impacted by the benefits of The IUL LASER Fund—and by our strategies for wealth, health, and life fulfillment—that he wanted to pass those along to others. As he looked to reenter the workforce, he realized he would rather engineer people's futures than aircraft, so he decided on a career change. He pursued his insurance licensing and joined our team.

Today, Karl Nelson takes pride in helping people have the peace of mind that comes from The IUL LASER Fund's liquidity, safety, predictable rates of return, tax advantages, and death benefit. He also relishes helping families embrace a holistic approach to Authentic Wealth in strategies like the KASH Blueprint and the Legacy Bank.

THE PRIMARY BENEFIT FOR ALL

As noted throughout Section I, anyone opening an IUL LASER Fund must establish a need for the death benefit, as it must be the primary reason for anyone to own an Indexed Universal Life policy. Before granting a policy, the insurance company's underwriters must determine and justify the death benefit based upon the economic loss that would be suffered by the beneficiary at the time of the application.

While most people don't anticipate passing along the income-tax-free death benefit to their heirs until later in life, as with Karl, it can be a much-needed boon to those left behind. Even when the insured passes away at an advanced age, the death benefit can bring critical financial security and opportunities to loved ones.

Unlike many other financial vehicles, the wealth transferred to heirs via an IUL LASER Fund's death benefit does so 100% income-tax-free, capital gains tax-free, and estate tax-free (for substantial estates to be estate tax-free, the death benefit must be structured properly through an Irrevocable Life Insurance Trust). Depending on the level of the death benefit at the time of the passing, that can mean tens of thousands or even millions of dollars tax-free for heirs.

Whether you're looking to implement an IUL LASER Fund solely for the death benefit or for additional reasons, it's helpful to understand the death benefit's positive impact on your loved ones.

BROTHERLY LOVE

Doug and his brother, Sherm (his real name), were best of friends their entire lives. From their boyhood schemes to their grown-up adventures, they shared a deep bond and countless memories. In his 40s, Sherm wanted to start setting aside money for retirement, and he wanted the protection of a death benefit for his family, so he came to Doug to open an IUL LASER Fund. Initially Doug set about structuring the policy as he typically would, assessing the minimum death benefit based upon how much Sherm could afford to put into the policy to max fund it.

Then Doug stopped and thought, "Wait a minute. This is my brother. This is the guy that I go motorcycle riding with, river rafting with. In the event that something ever happens to Sherm, I would wish I had helped him get as much as possible for his wife and children." So Doug proposed that Sherm add a term rider to double the death benefit, which would also allow him to sock away more money when he could afford to do so.

After putting the policy into place and doubling the death benefit, Doug didn't think much more about it—until his phone rang at 11:45 pm, March 10, 1999. It was Sherm's wife, Sue, sobbing. The highway patrol had just left their home, informing her that Sherm had been killed in a one-car rollover. Doug was devastated. With his best friend gone, too soon at age 50, the one consolation was that Sherm's family would be financially secure.

Doug recalled, "That doubling of the death benefit has allowed his sweet wife to live in dignity and provide religious mission and college funds for their kids. She put the death benefit into an IUL LASER Fund of her own, and she has been living comfortably on more than double the annual income (tax-free) that Social Security or his benefits at work would have provided." While Doug could not save his brother from a fatal accident, he is grateful he was able to empower Sherm's family to carry on in his absence, exemplifying his loving legacy.

WISH LISTS AND BEST WISHES

Joe Taylor (throughout the rest of this section, names and some details have been changed for privacy, unless otherwise noted) was an insurance agent for a national company known for home, life, and auto insurance. While Joe proudly represented his company, he knew the company's life insurance options were more traditional—they couldn't provide the range of benefits, tax-free retirement income, or rates of return an IUL LASER Fund could. He and his wife, in their mid-30s at the time, met with Doug to initiate IUL LASER Funds.

As the couple came in for annual reviews over the years, Doug was able to keep abreast of not just their policies' growth, but also their family and life experiences. One annual review, however, brought different news. Linda Taylor had late-stage cancer, with just over a year to live. Doug will never forget sitting with the Taylors as Linda, having undergone chemo and radiation, expressed that despite her sorrow she had peace of mind knowing her death benefit would make things easier on her family. And the Taylors had one request—they wanted to make the most of their time together, so they decided to borrow money on their policies for travel.

Doug could not have been happier to help them arrange the tax-free loans, and he was thrilled to hear how their adventures were going. They were able to visit places that had long been on their wish list, experiences they would not have been able to afford had they not had instant, liquid access to money in their policies.

In the annual reviews since her passing, Joe, now in his 60s, continues to share his relief and gratitude that they implemented IUL LASER Fund policies all those years back. Not only did those policies empower Linda and him to share unforgettable travel experiences, but they also enabled Joe to pay off remaining medical bills and expenses. There was even enough left over from her income-tax-free death benefit to open another IUL LASER Fund, which will fuel his upcoming retirement with additional tax-free income.

ENSURING THEIR FUTURE

Gary Lowell was heading into his retirement years when he came to us a few years ago. He was concluding a successful career; had been prudent with his earnings; and had invested in multiple high net-worth assets. He wanted to set aside a portion of his money into an IUL LASER Fund, strictly as a death benefit for his heirs.

Specifically, he wanted to move $750,000 from a brokerage account into an IUL LASER Fund. Gary was tired of the ups and downs of the market, and he wasn't thrilled with the hits that account had taken over the last several years. He wanted to park that $750,000 in an IUL LASER Fund, safely protected from the downturns in the market, earning a predictable rate of return. And he wanted the reassurance of knowing that money would pass on to his heirs as an income-tax-free death benefit.

To remain in compliance with TAMRA, Gary needed to transfer the money incrementally, over the next five years. So we helped him develop a plan to move the $750,000 from the brokerage account into an IUL LASER Fund over five years' time. The IUL LASER Fund will continue to earn interest until the time of Gary's passing, at which point his death benefit (currently at $1.8 million) will transfer to his heirs income-tax-free.

LIFE-CHANGING DECISIONS

Things had always been tight for the Millers. Starting out as a young couple, kids and responsibilities came fast, with no extra time or money to pursue a college degree. But Brian had always hoped to be able to do more for his family, and in his 40s he realized his dream of going back to school to become a chiropractor.

As he launched his practice, he couldn't believe how much he enjoyed going to work. He loved making a difference for his patients and was looking forward to making this second career last well into his 70s. He and his wife, Lisa, were thrilled; life was now taking the shape they'd always longed for. They were able to buy a new home, help their children (now in college and starting their career), travel, and save for retirement.

Brian and Lisa opened an IUL LASER Fund, designing it to receive ongoing annual payments of approximately $100,000 for the next twenty years. After their second annual payment, however, Brian learned that he had terminal brain cancer.

With just three months to live, he and Lisa made the most of their time together with their children. It was heartbreaking to watch their sorrow, but also a relief to see their calm, knowing that Lisa would receive an income-tax-free death benefit of $3.5 million. Brian was grateful he had set things in motion so his wife and family would be financially secure in his absence.

After Brian's passing, Lisa was able to use part of the death benefit to pay bills and living expenses, and she put the rest into a new IUL LASER Fund that will provide tax-free income for the rest of her life—and an income-tax-free death benefit for her children when she eventually passes.

If the Millers had chosen a traditional financial vehicle, that $200,000 they set aside—at even a stellar 10% or 20% growth rate over two years—would have left Lisa with under $250,000 (with taxes due, to boot). Instead, she received $3.5 million, income-tax-free. She's able to put that money to work to provide a comfortable life, with up to $200,000 tax-free income a year for the rest of her life, and ultimately, a valuable death benefit to leave as a legacy for her family.

BEST LAID PLANS

Ralph Baker was self-employed, in his 50s, when he met with Doug to create a plan for retirement. Based on Ralph's financial situation, Doug recommended an IUL LASER Fund policy. Ralph explained that he already had a mandatory life insurance policy through his union, and he didn't think he could afford—or need—any more insurance. When Doug learned how low Ralph's current death benefit was, he joked, "Frankly, the amount of insurance you have, if you died, you don't want to be dead very long."

Ralph laughed, reassuring him, "Doug, I'm fit as a bull moose, like Teddy Roosevelt." Despite Ralph's initial hesitation, after exploring his options he agreed the cost of insurance would be miniscule compared to the rate of return his policy would likely be averaging. He moved ahead with an IUL LASER Fund as a key retirement financial vehicle.

Doug recalled working on the life insurance application with Ralph, who, despite a nagging cough, did seem as strong as that bull moose. The day the insurance company approved Ralph's policy, Doug received a call from Ralph, asking if there were any way to quadruple the death benefit. Doug thought he was joking, since throughout the application process Ralph had insisted on getting the lowest possible death benefit. Doug explained, "That would mean you'd have to reapply. Are you serious? What's going on?"

Ralph sighed and said, "I was just diagnosed with fourth stage Hodgkin's Disease. The reason I was coughing? Turns out I have cancer. They give me about a year."

Unfortunately reapplying for a higher death benefit was now out of the question, but needless to say, as Ralph cherished his final thirteen months with his wife and family, he was grateful he hadn't passed up the opportunity to set aside money in a financial vehicle that would now be providing a critical death benefit for his loved ones. When Doug later delivered the death benefit to Ralph's family, he said it was a privilege to pass along the money that would allow Ralph's wife and children to continue doing the things that Ralph would have provided for, had he been able to live.

WHAT CAN GO WRONG

The primary reason for anyone to open an IUL LASER Fund is the death benefit, but sometimes it may be difficult to keep that in perspective when the desire to spend money on other things obscures the vision. The consequences of losing that perspective, however, can be damaging. Throughout these chapters, we will include a snapshot of client experiences where for one reason or another, they did not stick to their plan and their IUL LASER Fund goals suffered. These stories are offered as cautionary tales to help you avoid similar missteps.

Bruce Leavitt opened an IUL LASER Fund policy, designed with a $600,000 premium bucket and a $2 million death benefit. He was in the middle of the funding process when he remarried and had a son. His new wife was not thrilled with the idea of money going toward a life insurance policy, when she would rather have the cash on hand. She argued that her husband was so healthy, he wouldn't die any time soon, and they would have many more years to plan for retirement.

Bruce stuck to his original plan and continued funding the policy for another year or so, but he eventually acquiesced. He paid the surrender charges and cancelled his policy, pulling all his money out. Not long after, the unthinkable happened. While hunting, Bruce was fatally shot by another hunter who mistook him for an animal rustling in the bushes.

Not only was his death a shock and devastating loss for his family, but his wife was now left behind without financial security. Had they maintained the policy, she would have had millions of income-tax-free death benefit to empower her to raise her son in relative comfort. But without the policy, she could not afford to maintain their lifestyle and eventually had to move back home to live with her parents.

TIMELY BENEFITS

No matter the situation or size of the policy, IUL LASER Funds can clearly provide critical financial support at the time of the insured's passing. Whether starting an IUL LASER Fund with additional objectives in mind (such as retirement income or business planning) or solely for the death benefit, if structured and managed properly, in the end every IUL LASER Fund becomes an income-tax-free blessing to those left behind. With the additional liquidity, safety, rate of return and tax advantages, it is an invaluable tool in life, and yes, even in death.

3

Retirement Planning

As a successful tax accountant, Rob Mitchell was the kind of guy who managed his money well. For years, he had been setting aside money in traditional financial vehicles to build a retirement nest egg. When he discovered The IUL LASER Fund approach, he researched the strategies in-depth and was intrigued by the unique liquidity, safety, predictable rates of return, and tax advantages. He ultimately decided to reposition some of his money into policies for him and his wife.

At age 56, he transitioned $400,000 into a policy with one insurance company, and another $400,000 into a second policy with a different insurance company, each policy with a $1.2 million death benefit. He chose to go with two companies to diversify his portfolio, taking advantage of specific policy features and indexes at each company. The Mitchells fully funded their policies in the initial five years, during which time the two policies averaged a rate of return of 8.61% interest.

Since they have ample income elsewhere, they are not taking any tax-free income from these policies. They have designated their IUL LASER Funds purely for retirement planning, which means the money in the policies is free to continue to compound at full value. When they retire in a few years, they will be able to take a healthy annual income from their policies until they pass on, at which time their heirs will receive a tax-free death benefit. The Mitchells couldn't be more pleased.

AN IUL LASER RETIREMENT

In addition to the death benefit, retirement planning is perhaps the most common objective for those with IUL LASER Funds. It is among the safest of places to set aside money—the guaranteed floor of 0% provides assurance that even in the worst of economic climates, you won't lose money due to market volatility. The IUL LASER Fund's predictable rates of return afford a good gauge of the pace of growth you can expect. The liquidity can be empowering. Even for those like the Mitchells who don't plan on taking any income from their policies before retirement, the knowledge that you can access money at any time, for an emergency or other need, is reassuring.

And perhaps the biggest reason so many turn to The IUL LASER Fund for retirement planning are the tax-free advantages. As explained in Section I, the income you take from an IUL LASER Fund is not deemed earned, portfolio, or passive income—which according to Section 7702 of the Internal Revenue Code, are the only types of income currently subject to income tax. So any money you borrow properly from your policy is income-tax-free. And when you pass on, your heirs receive a death benefit, income-tax-free.

This can make a significant financial difference. Compare The IUL LASER Fund scenario to many Americans relying on traditional financial vehicles and Social Security during retirement. Because they have lost many of their former tax deductions (dependents, business expenses, etc.), they often find themselves in a tax bracket that is as high or higher than during their earning years. They often need to downgrade their retirement dreams to stretch their dollars and avoid outliving their money. And when it comes to transferring wealth at death, there is often less to pass along than what they had hoped, and what they do pass on comes with tax consequences.

THE INCOME POWER OF TWO FUNDS

At age 60, Ben Coleman could see retirement just over the horizon, and he decided to open an IUL LASER Fund. He wanted to move $780,000 into the policy, a combination of money from regular income and funds in a taxable account (where performance was lackluster and taxes took a regular bite). The policy started with a $1,875,000 death benefit.

He had planned on funding the policy over five years, but there were a few delays. Thanks to The IUL LASER Fund's flexibility, that was not a problem. He ended up fully funding it in six years, and like the Mitchells, Ben will not touch any money in the policy until he retires. He opened the policy strictly for retirement planning and eventual wealth transfer to his children through the income-tax-free death benefit. So far, it has earned as much as 17% annual interest, with an average annual rate of return of 7.8%.

A couple years ago, Ben remarried. He opened a second IUL LASER Fund, with a $600,000 premium bucket. With retirement income a priority, they chose a policy that does not pay out a death benefit until the second spouse passes on, which reduces costs. He pays $10,000 a month into the policy, and plans to fully fund it in five years. Between the two policies, Ben and his wife will be able to take an annual tax-free income of $150,000 to $200,000 when they retire. For Ben, the ability to earn a predictable rate of return, to know that his money is safe, and to look forward to a robust annual income—free of income taxes—provides a much brighter future than his previous approach. This is a retirement he can really look forward to.

FOR EXPENSES AND VACATIONS

Joan Campbell was in her late 50s and her husband, Rich, was in his early 60s when they created IUL LASER Funds. Joan's policy was designed to hold $200,000, and Rich's was designed for $250,000, both with a $600,000 death benefit.

Although they had originally intended to maximum fund the policies, they stopped adding funds when each policy was about 75% full. (Note: You don't have to fully fund policies to utilize them for needs like death benefit or income. However, partially funding an IUL LASER Fund could affect the net rate of return after policy charges, which could impact maximum growth potential.)

Now in retirement, the Campbells don't use their policies for regular income—instead they access money in their policies for various expenses, as needed. One year they may borrow $12,000 from Joan's policy to pay taxes. Another year they may borrow $20,000 from Rich's policy to take the family on vacation.

For the Campbells, their IUL LASER Funds provide peace of mind during retirement. They know their money is safe from economic downturns. They can watch it grow (their policies are averaging an annual rate of 8%), and they love having the ability to dip into their policies to cover the cost of occasional necessities and create memorable opportunities for the family to connect.

A LITTLE GOES A LONG WAY

When Colby was in his early 20s, he decided to follow in his parents' footsteps. They had opened IUL LASER Funds several years earlier, and now as a young adult, Colby wanted to start one of his own. Still in school and on a limited budget, the policy's premium bucket was just $10,000, with a $100,000 death benefit. He paid what he could into the policy every month, $50 to $75.

When Colby married a few years later, he and his wife opened a similar policy on her—a $10,000 premium bucket with a $100,000 death benefit. Eventually those policies were funded, and after graduate school, when money was more plentiful, he opened a third IUL LASER Fund, this one with a $100,000 premium bucket and a $720,000 death benefit. With a young family, he typically paid just $500 a month into the policy, planning on funding it over ten years. After the sale of some property, however, they were able to finish funding the policy earlier than anticipated, in its sixth year.

With rates of return on their polices averaging 7% to 9%, they feel content knowing they have money working for them in safe financial vehicles that they can turn to for tax-free income during retirement. They appreciate knowing if an emergency arises, they can borrow money from their policies. And still in their 30s, with the death benefit in place, they feel reassured that should anything tragic occur, their growing family will have the financial means to continue moving forward.

FROM THEIR RETIREMENT TO HERS

When the Harolds created their IUL LASER Fund, they did so with the intent to enjoy a healthy tax-free income during retirement. But just as John retired, he passed away unexpectedly. While Helen was reeling from the loss, she was relieved to receive a significant death benefit. While many around her urged her to use the death benefit to pay off her mortgage and buy a new car with cash, she decided to create an IUL LASER Fund for herself.

She wanted to perpetuate The IUL LASER Fund's benefits for herself— liquidity, safety, predictable rates of return and tax advantages—as she faced her golden years alone. She understood that her IUL LASER Fund would provide the means to pay off any mortgage or debts should she need to, and that she would be gaining far more with her money at work in her policy, with its safety and predictable rates of return, than paying off her debts immediately.

Over the years, Helen has been able to live comfortably on the tax-free income she borrows from her policy. She uses tax-free income from her policy to pay for everything from her mortgage to her car loan (which she was able to procure at just 1% interest). She has been able to help her nieces and nephews pay for college tuition and religious missions, and she also has the means to care for her aging mother. While it is not the retirement she envisioned sharing with John, her retirement years have been filled with opportunity and abundance, for which Helen could not be more grateful.

WHAT CAN GO WRONG

The IUL LASER Fund is a long-term financial vehicle designed to provide an income-tax-free death benefit—with the opportunity to provide other benefits like tax-free income during retirement. Its success, however, depends heavily on a key factor … you. When you practice strong financial habits, it can perform as planned. When you succumb to less-than-responsible temptations, you can veer off course.

The Kerrs, for example, established an IUL LASER Fund during their late 50s. In addition to their upcoming pensions and Social Security, they wanted to utilize an IUL LASER Fund to supplement their retirement income. We worked with them to design a policy that would provide about $30,000 in annual tax-free income.

They were disciplined, sending their payments in each year to maximum fund their policy, coming in for their annual reviews, staying on track with their retirement goals. At age 65, they said good-bye to work and turned to their nest eggs, enjoying their pensions, Social Security, and tax-free IUL LASER Fund income.

Before long, they had an opportunity arise. They were offered all kinds of wealth if they invested in joining a startup direct sales company. It would require hundreds of thousands of dollars. They debated what to do, but eventually could not resist. They pulled out the maximum amount possible from their policy, promising themselves to repay the loan as soon as their direct sales fortunes came in.

What sounded too good to pass up ended up being too good to be true. The company went up in smoke, with their IUL LASER Fund turning to ashes. They simply did not have the money to repay the loan on their policy. While loans are not necessarily due during the life of the policy, if you take the maximum amount and do not add any more money to the policy, eventually the policy charges can nibble away and cause the policy to lapse. They also did not have a Loan Protection Rider, which can at least protect the death benefit in cases like this. (For more on the Loan Protection Rider and how it can protect your policy, see Section I, Chapter 8.)

This is exactly what the Kerrs allowed their policy to do. It was with a heavy heart that they expressed regret over losing sight of their goals, chasing new opportunities, and losing out on tax-free retirement income that would have helped make their retirement more abundant.

A SECURE FUTURE

When looking ahead to retirement, The IUL LASER Fund can provide powerful peace of mind. With its guaranteed safety, you never have to fear an economic storm will blow your money away due to market volatility. The predictable rates of return can help your money grow toward a stable financial future. The liquidity affords you the ability to borrow money from your policy for expenses or regular income, and the income-tax-free advantages support you in making the most of *your* money.

4

Working Capital

Hank Freeman makes his money flipping real estate. Not just a house or two at a time—he purchases large-scale real estate like strip malls and apartment complexes, renovates them, sells them, and makes a handsome profit. Hank and his wife have four IUL LASER Funds, from which Hank borrows working capital to fund real estate ventures.

There are times when he buys an apartment complex that has fallen into disrepair and vacancy rates are high. The owners may be behind on their mortgage or just unable to maintain the property properly. He borrows money from one of his policies to cover the down payment or earnest money on the property, say $1 million or more. He simply submits the form for the loan to the insurance company, has the money wired from his IUL LASER Funds to his bank account, and is ready to move forward.

He also uses his policies as collateral to secure construction loans to cover the cost of renovations. Usually within about a year, he sells the restored property at a profit.

The former owners are relieved to be free of the once-struggling property; the tenants are happy to be living in a better environment; the realtors involved in the transactions are making sizable commissions; the new owners are pleased to pick up a thriving real estate asset; and

Hank's net worth continues to grow. It's a win-win for everyone, made possible by his IUL LASER Funds.

When he completes each find-fix-flip cycle, Hank returns the money he borrowed right back into his IUL LASER Funds. This has become a well he can return to time and again, and he does, to his great advantage.

WORKING CAPITAL

Thousands of savvy professionals use IUL LASER Funds for working capital, because it provides significant advantages over traditional methods. When saving, you typically set aside the money you use for short-term business needs in a business savings account. Yes, this provides liquid access to cash when needed, but you're earning just 1% to 2% on the money in the account. When you need to fund a project or acquisition, that interest rate goes down to 0% on any money you pull out, and when you put the money back in, you're back up to just 1% to 2% interest.

Instead, if you borrow from your IUL LASER Fund, you can come out ahead. As explained in Section I, Chapter 7, when you borrow money from your policy, that money is still technically in The IUL LASER Fund. So in this scenario, let's say your policy is earning an average rate of return of 7%, while the money you borrow is being charged 5% interest. You're averaging a 2% spread. Your money is STILL going to work for you. You're able to finance business ventures, without all the loan applications, red tape, and possible funding delays. The money you borrow is tax-free; and all your money (that is still in your IUL LASER Fund) can continue growing tax-deferred. You're moving forward with your venture quickly and easily.

CONTINUED DEVELOPMENT

Joe Sherman is a developer, specializing in residential homes and commercial lodging. Since discovering IUL LASER Funds, he has changed his business model. He has seized the opportunity to have policies providing life insurance for him and his wife—and he puts those policies to work providing working capital for his developments.

Over the last few years, he has borrowed money from their policies for several projects. Sometimes it has been for short-term needs, such as borrowing money to secure a lot, and then putting the money right back into his policy thirty days later when his construction loan comes through. Other times, he has borrowed enough to finance an entire construction project, putting the money back into his policies when the build is done and the property sells.

Using this approach, Joe has made an additional $100,000 or more in interest than he would have using the traditional savings account method for working capital. The liquidity and predictable rates of return in his IUL LASER Funds enables Joe to look to continued growth, with the opportunity to make money on both his real estate deals, and his insurance policies.

LENDING SUCCESS

Not only do Bobby Collins's IUL LASER Fund policies provide the reassurance of an income-tax-free death benefit for him and his wife, they also provide a business opportunity. Bobby has leveraged his IUL LASER Funds to become something of a commercial bank himself.

Bobby extends short-term loans to contractors at 16% to 18% interest. He borrows the money from his policies to lend the contractors, and returns the money to the policies as soon as they repay their loans.

Think about it; Bobby is borrowing money from his policies, currently at about 5% interest. Because his IUL LASER Fund is earning an average of 7% interest, the money he borrows is still averaging a 2% spread. That same chunk of money he turns around and lends to contractors—that is earning another 16% to 18% interest.

Over the past several years, Bobby has made millions doing this. He has done so with peace of mind knowing that he has life insurance policies in force should anything happen to him or his wife. He has enjoyed the liquidity and income-tax-free advantages of harnessing a rewarding business opportunity through his IUL LASER Funds.

WHEN OPPORTUNITY KNOCKS

The Butlers opened an IUL LASER Fund to ensure they would have an income-tax-free death benefit in place, as well as money for retirement. After fully funding their first policy, they opened a second—and then a business opportunity arose.

It was a real estate deal where they could contribute $300,000 and earn 9% annually. They decided to take the opportunity, so they borrowed $300,000 from their policies at 4% interest ($12,000). That same year, both policies earned close to 10% interest. Between what they were charged in interest and what that money earned in interest, their IUL LASER Funds netted $18,000. That same $300,000, put to work in the real estate deal, earned $27,000. Altogether, in the one year they made $45,000 on that $300,000—a 15% return.

Say they had pulled the $300,000 out of a traditional savings account, they would have earned only 9% in the real estate deal. If they had with-drawn the money from a 401(k), they would have paid taxes, and an additional 10% penalty for being under age 59½. Thanks to the flexibility, liquidity and tax-free advantages of their IUL LASER Funds, they were able to take advantage of the opportunity—and make significantly more than if they had funded the opportunity some other way.

FLEXIBILITY AND TAX-FREE CAPITAL

Larry Fulton had opened an IUL LASER Fund with a $300,000 premium bucket for the income-tax-free death benefit, and for its capabilities as a tax-free working capital account. In structuring the policy, he added a rider that would provide him full liquidity in the early years with no surrender charges. He knew this would add a bit of expense and affect values over the life of the policy, but it gave him the advantages he needed for a working capital account.

He began to put $80,000 a year into his IUL LASER Fund, and at the start of his third year of funding, he borrowed $180,000 tax-free from the policy for a business venture. He paid back the loan within three months. For his next venture, he borrowed $90,000 tax-free. He is currently re-paying that loan on an amortized schedule he created, paying himself interest like he would a bank. He did not need to do this, but he likes the sense of self-discipline and financial growth it creates. As he looks to the future, he is grateful for the flexibility and opportunities his IUL LASER Fund affords him to build his business.

WHAT CAN GO WRONG

Properly funding an IUL LASER Fund according to the design of the policy is crucial to the success of the policy. If circumstances change, unless you work with your IUL specialist to make adjustments to your policy, you'll get less-than-optimal results.

Cliff Wharton was interested in creating an IUL LASER Fund with a $100,000 premium bucket to use for working capital, along with a death benefit. He put his first $20,000 into the policy, and within a week, pulled out $16,000 tax-free for a business venture.

Ideally it is beneficial to fund the policy more before pulling the majority of the money out, but it is not imperative. To complicate things, over the next few years, he did not continue funding the policy. He would just sprinkle a few dollars in here and there to cover the policy charges and keep the policy from lapsing.

Thirty years later, his policy is still in force, but it has essentially become term insurance. Because he did not continue funding the policy to at least 50% full or more—it cannot provide all the benefits he had hoped for. It is merely limping along, and thankfully, will at least be able to provide a modest income-tax-free death benefit upon his passing.

DOUBLE TIME

For those who are engaged in business ventures that require working capital, The IUL LASER Fund provides unique advantages. The liquidity and flexibility offer timely access to money. The tax-free nature of The IUL LASER Fund empowers you to use all of your money for the venture, without splitting it with Uncle Sam first. And the ability to borrow money from your IUL LASER Fund, while still having it earn interest in the policy at predictable rates of return, gives you the rare ability to have your money working for you in two places at once.

5

School, Family, and Life

The Schooners' son, James, was preparing for medical school—an endeavor that would cost about $500,000. As James investigated traditional student loans, the family looked at an alternate solution, one that would be far more flexible and that could benefit everyone—son *and* parents.

Rather than going to the local bank, they decided to turn to their family's "Legacy Bank," utilizing money in the Schooners' IUL LASER Fund to cover medical school costs. They drew up an official contract that allowed James to borrow what he needed from his parents each year, which they in turn borrowed from their IUL LASER Fund at 5% interest, income-tax-free.

When James completed medical school, he began paying his parents back in monthly installments, at 7% interest—a rate James insisted on. While his parents were willing to offer the loan at no interest, James wanted to be repay them at a healthy market rate of 7% interest—as his way of thanking them. The Schooners put each monthly payment right back into their IUL LASER Fund, where it is currently contributing to the further growth of their policy's value.

Originally the Schooners opened their IUL LASER Fund for the death benefit and future retirement income, but they have been thrilled to discover it has so many more uses, including the ability to help their son attend medical school without the hassle, additional costs, and rigidity of traditional student loans.

FUNDING THE FAMILY'S ENDEAVORS

Many policyholders experience a similar joy in the versatility of The IUL LASER Fund. They leverage the money in their policy to fund the family's worthwhile endeavors, such as education, weddings, humanitarian and religious missions, even big vacations with extended family. The IUL LASER Fund becomes the generator for their family's Legacy Bank, empowering themselves, their children, and their grandchildren to pursue meaningful experiences.

The flexibility of The IUL LASER Fund is ideal in these situations. Remember, when you borrow money from an IUL LASER Fund, repaying those loans is optional. As discussed throughout Section I, loans on IUL LASER Funds are not due during your lifetime, and are cleared away upon your death. That said, many policyholders choose to incorporate some type of system for repayment, to instill a sense of accountability in family members—and to replenish and maximize the future value of the Alternate Loan.

When you borrow from your IUL LASER Fund with an Alternate Loan, the money in the insurance policy continues to earn the indexed rate (which in this example averages 5% to 10% tax-deferred), and the insurance company charges you interest at a lower rate, say 5%. Essentially, you are averaging a 2% spread on the borrowed amount (assuming you're earning an average 7% return). And if you repay those loans, your IUL LASER Fund value benefits even more. (For more on Alternate Loans, see Section I, Chapter 8.)

Looking at the Schooners, while their son was in school, they borrowed a total of $500,000 from their policy at 5% interest, tax-free, to lend him. That money was still earning an average of 7% interest a year in their policy, based on index performance. So they were averaging a 2% spread each year on the borrowed amount.

Their son is now repaying the loans at 7% interest. When they eventual-ly get all the money back in the insurance policy, part of their son's 7% interest is paying back that 5% interest they were being charged on that loan. Which means, over time, it will be as if they never had lent their son any money anyway. And in fact, they will come out a little ahead. Was that their goal? No, they would have lent him the money at 0% interest, but their son wanted to show his appreciation and help add to their IUL LASER Fund once he was earning a handsome salary as a doctor.

You can set up the way your family approaches your Legacy Bank in whatever way works best for you. If repayment is part of the arrange-ment, it is important to put things in writing and for everyone involved to honor that agreement as you would any professional contract. Obviously there can be flexibility if circumstances change. Say, for instance, James Schooner had a delay in finding employment after medical school. They could have postponed repayment until he was settled in his career.

And that is one of the many beauties of an IUL LASER Fund—the ability to access money when needed (liquidity), the tax-free loans (tax advan-tages), and the opportunity to repay loans as works best for the situation.

CREATING A LEGACY

Richard Hambert had worked hard throughout his life. By the time he re-tired, he had amassed a net worth well over $20 million. Just a few years into retirement, he established an IUL LASER Fund and chartered his fam-ily's Legacy Bank. He outlined a KASH Blueprint (as explained in Section II, Chapter 1,) creating clear parameters for how his family could access money from the Legacy Bank, incentivizing positive pursuits, and rein-forcing greater accountability among his children and grandchildren. He also changed his trust from one of equal distribution to equal opportunity.

Richard uses his IUL LASER Fund to support his grandchildren's educa-tion, which they can access for a bachelor's, master's, and doctoral de-gree. But he does not cover the entire tuition. To help them get some skin in the game, his grandchildren are required to come up with 50% of the costs, which he then matches.

Richard is a romantic at heart, and he believes young couples benefit more from kick starting their lives together with a meaningful honeymoon, rather than a lavish wedding. So his KASH Rules of Governance allow for a $5,000 wedding gift—if it's used for the honeymoon, to cement the relationship.

When it comes to real estate, Richard matches dollar-for-dollar what his children and grandchildren save for their first real estate acquisition—but with one caveat. As a strong believer in the 3 Dimensions of Authentic Wealth and the importance of gaining at least a foundational understanding of financial strategies, Richard requires that they attend one of our events and read at least one of our books.

Richard has seen an evolution in his family since implementing his KASH Blueprint—a greater accountability and sense of personal investment in pursuing goals and achievements. His IUL LASER Fund has become a powerful tool for granting equal opportunity to his family members. And he is encouraged about the legacy, habits, and values he will eventually be leaving behind.

A PRIVATE EDUCATION

The Bradfords practice financial self-discipline. They work hard, and they consistently live on less than they earn. While not wildly wealthy, they have been prudent with their money and have opened several IUL LASER Funds over the years.

As big believers in the power of education, they have used those IUL LASER Funds for their children's private schooling. By borrowing tax-free from their policies, they have been able to pay for top-notch educations for their children from elementary through junior high and high school. Their children are now attending a private university, preparing for successful careers after college.

All of this has been possible because they systematically socked away money into IUL LASER Funds. As they look ahead to retirement in about twenty years, they have the reassurance of knowing they will also be able to access tax-free income, and eventually leave an income-tax-free death benefit for their children when they pass on.

HELPING LOVED ONES

With an eye toward future retirement income, the Johnsons opened two IUL LASER Fund policies while in their 50s. When Sam passed away about fifteen years later, Elaine was able to take the money from his death benefit and open another IUL LASER Fund to continue the retirement income opportunities. She was relieved to know she would be secure financially, accessing income from their policies to cover not just her needs, but also to enjoy a good quality of life.

She has been able to repair and renovate her home, for example. And as for her family, Elaine has been able to ease financial burdens. One of their children has a special needs child, and Elaine has turned to her IUL LASER Funds to help provide for the medical costs and care her grand-child requires. She has also been able to assist other grandchildren with their schooling and other endeavors—all of which has brought her joy.

For Elaine, the Johnsons' IUL LASER Funds have provided for so much more than she and her husband had anticipated. Not only has the tax-free income provided peace of mind, but she has been empowered to help where her family needs it most.

PAYING FOR COLLEGE ... AND MORE

With two children heading to college and a third not far behind, the Reynolds were feeling a little anxious. While the kids' grandfather had more than enough to cover the cost of tuition, the Reynolds wanted to be more self-sufficient in funding their children's university education.

They consolidated debt, streamlined their cash flow, and created an IUL LASER Fund with about a $150,000 premium bucket they would fund over the next seven years. They are now able to borrow money tax-free from their policy to cover college expenses.

As a bonus, due to asset adjustments made during The IUL LASER Fund planning process, one of their children received scholarship and grant money totaling more than $120,000 from the private university he was hoping to attend. As they look ahead to retirement, they're also thrilled their IUL LASER Fund will supplement their income with over $20,000 a year, tax-free.

Finding a way to pay for college expenses was the original motivator, but in the end, opening an IUL LASER Fund brought multiple benefits. They have personal pride in empowering their children to pursue educational goals; they have a plan for tax-free supplemental retirement income; and they have a death benefit that will help their children when they pass on.

WHAT CAN GO WRONG

With grandchildren approaching their teen and college years, Mary Edwards liked the idea of creating a family Legacy Bank. She looked forward to helping her grandchildren with school, weddings, and other opportunities, so she opened an IUL LASER Fund.

As she began funding her policy, she was delighted by its liquidity. Perhaps too delighted. She would get excited about random ventures, such as building emergency kits, and she would borrow from the policy to pay for the new projects.

Despite warnings from her IUL specialist to slow the pace of her loans, she continued to borrow from the policy. Eventually she had borrowed so much (and she did not have a Loan Protection Rider, which we explain in more detail in Section I, Chapter 8), so her policy was in danger of lapsing. She ended up canceling her IUL LASER Fund. Had she maintained better financial discipline, she could have met her long-term goals, but unfortunately her short-term pursuits robbed her of the future she had envisioned.

A BOON TO FAMILIES

For those who maintain their future focus and properly utilize The IUL LASER Fund, it can make a significant difference in a family's approach to life. Not only can it provide the financial fuel for worthwhile pursuits, it can also be the motivator for adopting the family's values and vision. It can help families live with accountability and responsibility. It can be the antidote for entitlement that can sometimes otherwise plague families, as explored in Doug's book, *Entitlement Abolition*. Essentially, it can empower greater abundance.

6

Lump Sums

As owners of apartments and commercial buildings, David and Jane Soto had prospered in real estate. Now in their 50s, they had come to a point where they felt ready to move on. They had grown weary of tending to tenant needs and the rigors of property management over the years, so they sold their properties.

But they were faced with a dilemma. What to do with the significant lump sum of money they had just acquired through the sale of their real estate? They did not need the income yet, but they were leery of putting it in the market. Just shy of retirement years, they knew they could not afford the risk of a volatile market. While talking with friends, they learned about The IUL LASER Fund, which sparked their curiosity. The death benefit, along with the predictable rates of return and future tax-free retirement income sounded ideal. And the safety was exactly what they were looking for.

The Sotos decided this was the path for them. As it now stands, in another two years, they will have maximum funded their IUL LASER Fund with a $500,000 premium bucket and a death benefit of about $1.3 million.

In a few more years, when they are ready for retirement, they will be able to enjoy tax-free income, as well as money for helping their children with education and other needs. They are relieved to know their money is safe, earning predictable rates of return, and that they will have far better tax advantages than any other vehicle they had previously been considering.

THE LUMP SUM SOLUTION

Lump sums can be a blessed windfall for many, but they can also raise serious financial questions. The first: how do you help the money grow, without putting it at undue risk? There were many people whose lump sums went into the market and enjoyed growth for a time, then nearly disappeared during the Great Recession of 2008. The second: where can you put it that can ensure liquidity, and where it can be accessed tax-free, then transfer income-tax-free to heirs?

Traditional financial vehicles can pose challenges in each of these areas, which is why an IUL LASER Fund can be a godsend for folks who find themselves suddenly flush with cash. But The IUL LASER Fund does have its limitations.

If you want to structure your IUL LASER Fund to provide for tax-free access to the money—for retirement income or any of the other reasons illustrated throughout Section II—then you must take time to move the money into the policy. TAMRA dictates that funding the policy must be spread out over a minimum of five years to ensure those tax-free benefits.

But if your goal is primarily wealth transfer via the income-tax-free death benefit—and you are not looking to borrow money from your policy (or you don't mind paying taxes if you do)—then those limitations disappear.

As explained in Section I, Chapter 7, you can purposely violate TAMRA, fund it all at once, and your IUL LASER Fund is now termed a Modified Endowment Contract (MEC). Referring to the apartment building example in Section I, Chapter 5, it would be like leasing out the five-story apartment all at once. Instantly all five floors are available to turn a profit for you.

Your money in the MEC is growing tax-deferred, at an average rate of 5% to 10%. It's safe from downturns in the market, with a guaranteed floor of 0% even in the worst of times. When you pass away, your money blossoms into an income-tax-free death benefit as it passes along to your beneficiaries. And in the case that you may want to access money in your policy, you can—you will simply pay taxes on it like you would an annuity.

However you structure and fund it, IUL LASER Funds provide an excellent vehicle for lump sums that come your way. And for many people, they provide much more than just financial benefits.

FROM DEATH BENEFIT TO LIVING BENEFITS

Barbara Heaton was recently widowed. Her husband had left behind a $2 million death benefit from a life insurance policy, and she had parked the big lump sum in a savings account at her local bank. She would need the money to pay the bills and take care of her family, and she was hoping it would last her a good long while. Sure it was earning less than 1% interest, but at least it was safe, with no fees, so she figured that was best.

As a mother with teenagers at home and her first couple grandchildren living nearby, she was still very involved in the thick of life, with little time to think much beyond the day-to-day. Then she came to one of our firm's events, where she started to consider that there may be better alternatives than the savings account. Incidentally, she also brought along one of her younger sons who was just graduating from high school to learn about the 3 Dimensions of Authentic Wealth, accountability, and dealing "above the line"—something she later said helped her son turn around his less than-optimal teenage approach to life.

Barbara decided she wanted to get more out of that $2 million than what the bank could offer. She transferred her money into two IUL LASER Fund policies over the next five years, much like the Sotos.

Now, she is able to take tax-free retirement income from those IUL LASER Funds. She is grateful for the flexibility, liquidity, safety, predictable rates of return and tax advantages her IUL LASER Funds have provided, especially since she realizes that by now, had she left the $2 million in the savings account, it would be dwindling. Instead, that money will continue to provide for her needs until she ultimately passes away, at which time she will be able to leave behind an income-tax-free death benefit to her family.

PASSING ON A LEGACY

The Bannisters were in their 60s when they opened two IUL LASER Funds. They had a sizable amount of net worth, much of which they wanted to tuck into IUL LASER Funds. They had pensions that would be providing for the majority of their retirement income in the next few years, so they were drawn to IUL LASER Funds primarily for the death benefit and occasional access to their money, as needed.

The IUL LASER Funds would provide an excellent income-tax-free way to transfer their wealth to their posterity—and with eight children and a growing posse of grandchildren, they had a significant posterity to consider.

Sooner than expected, Fred passed away within a few years. Shelly Bannister received a lump sum from his death benefit—and she knew exactly what she wanted to do with it. She opened another IUL LASER Fund so it could continue to grow and eventually pass on to her children.

Today, she uses her IUL LASER Fund for tax-free income—and for things that bring her joy. She has established a family Legacy Bank, which her grandchildren can access for education. And she takes her children and grandchildren on unforgettable Family Retreats with a Purpose (as discussed in Section II, Chapter 1). On these getaways, she loves passing along the Bannisters' Vision & Values and maintaining the family's close-knit unity that would make her husband proud. She feels reassured that when she passes on, not only will she be able to transfer her death benefit on to her children, but the money from the additional policy she created with the lump sum from Fred's death benefit, as well.

FACING LIFE ON HER OWN

After Grace Humphrey lost her husband in a tragic accident, she received $300,000 from a liability insurance settlement. She was in her early 60s, missing her husband, and trying to sort out how she would approach the coming years on her own. She wanted to make sure she could not only preserve that lump sum, but also leverage it for as much retirement income as possible.

She opened an IUL LASER Fund with a $300,000 premium bucket and an $800,000 income-tax-free death benefit. As a financially disciplined woman, she made ends meet with other income so she could funnel the entire $300,000 to her policy over the next five years.

Since then, Grace has enjoyed regular tax-free income from her policy. She has also been able to borrow additional money from her policy on three or four occasions for things like home repairs and trips with her children and grandchildren.

Grace could not be more pleased with the safety The IUL LASER Fund has provided her lump sum settlement, as well as the liquidity for tax-free income that has helped her make the most of her golden years as a widow. She is grateful she will also have an income-tax-free death benefit to pass along to her family when she eventually reunites with her husband.

WHAT CAN GO WRONG

Several years ago, a large mining company offered an alternative to a 401(k) plan—it was essentially a matching program for employees who wanted to open IUL LASER Funds. The policies were structured for modest long-term contributions, and employees could automatically direct $100 in after-tax dollars each month to their policies. The company would then match the contribution. To help cover the cost of taxes on the match, the company "grossed up the match," which means if an employee were in a 25% tax bracket, for example, the company would put $133 into the policy.

Tragically, the mine suffered a catastrophic accident, and several dozen miners lost their lives. Fortunately because many of those miners had been utilizing The IUL LASER Fund plan, their families received income-tax-free death benefits. If those workers had been using a traditional 401(k) plan, their families would have received far less.

One of the widows, Dorothy Hampton, decided to use the $200,000 lump sum she had received in an income-tax-free death benefit to create an IUL LASER Fund of her own. This way the money could not only provide a death benefit for her children someday, but it also enabled tax-advantaged growth, liquidity, and safety on that $200,000.

Not long after she had begun funding the policy, she remarried. Her new husband wanted to start a restaurant, and he had his eye on the money in the policy for startup capital. Dorothy decided to take out as much money from the policy as she could to launch his restaurant. We reminded her the policy would take a hit, and she would need to make payments to cover the cost of the insurance. Despite the warnings, she proceeded with her plan, promising herself she would repay the loans just as soon as the restaurant succeeded (which he assured her it would).

Within about a year, the restaurant had gone belly up, the new husband had left her, and Dorothy did not have enough money to maintain the policy (and no Loan Protection Rider, which as explained in Section I, Chapter 8, could have helped protect the policy), so, sadly, she let it lapse. If she had taken out less than the maximum loan, and/or she had made payments, she would not have had to let the policy go.

SUMMING IT UP

When lump sums come along, whether through business deals, the sale of real estate, a death benefit, or other means, when handled right, The IUL LASER Fund can provide a safe, tax-advantaged path for making even more of that lump sum. You can choose to maximum fund an IUL LASER Fund over five or more years—or if wealth transfer is a primary goal, you can fund it all at once, create a MEC, and enjoy all the liquidity, safety, predictable rates of return, and income-tax-free death benefits that an IUL LASER Fund provides.

Business Planning

When Kate Laramy's husband passed away from an accident, she was devastated—not only was she facing life without Ken, but she would now be a single mother raising six children. Unfortunately Ken did not have a personal life insurance policy that could have left her an income-tax-free death benefit. She was worried how she would make ends meet long-term.

Then she learned she would be receiving $1 million from a policy her husband's business had opened on Ken for this very reason. She discovered that as part of their business planning, both Ken and his partner had life insurance policies in place as part of a buy-sell agreement. Should either partner pass away prematurely, the life insurance policy would serve to "buy out" the deceased partner's share of the company. This would empower the remaining partner to proceed with full ownership of the company, and serve to help the deceased partner's family with a valuable tax-free lump sum.

In Kate's case it was some of the best news she had received in a long time. She decided to open an IUL LASER Fund policy with the money, and she has been able to move forward, knowing she will have enough to provide for her children and enjoy a good quality of life throughout the rest of her years.

INSURANCE FOR BUSINESS PLANNING

The IUL LASER Fund can be used for exactly this type of buy-sell agreement, which makes for an excellent "exit strategy" in business planning. Whether partners decide to leave the company, they pass away, or they become disabled, the insurance compensates the remaining partner with money to buy out the company. In the case of death, most attorneys will arrange for the money to go directly to the widow, so it can be possibly transferred tax-free, helping the widow avoid capital gains tax on the "sale" of the business. And it also helps make the transition simple, without the widow "inheriting" partnership in the business and having to decide if he or she wants to take on running a company—and helps the remaining partner avoid the awkwardness of deciding if that's even plausible.

The IUL LASER Fund can also be used for business planning in the form of "key person insurance." Here, The IUL LASER Fund is used to cover the economic value of a key person in a business. For example, if a CEO is integral to a company's brand or financial success and were to suddenly die, the policy provides tax-free capital to be transferred to the business, to help the company recover from the loss of the primary figure in the business.

This strategy can be valuable for many companies, large and small. There are also options in how it can be structured. While some companies may choose to maximum fund the policy, other companies choose to minimum fund the policy for the maximum amount of death benefit they desire. (In this case, the goal is to keep costs low.)

What's more, should the key person reach retirement alive and well, the policy ownership can be transferred to the key person, who can then choose to maximum fund the policy and name her or his loved ones as beneficiaries. At this point, the key person can use The IUL LASER Fund in all the same ways we are describing in Section II—for an income-tax-free death benefit for the family, as well as living benefits, such as retirement income, working capital for future business ventures, etc.

LEAVING A LEGACY FOR EMPLOYEES

Bill Zimmerman (his real name) was always fascinated by personal financial planning and investments. He started reading "The Wall Street Journal" in high school and majored in economics and accounting in college. Shortly after finishing college, he joined the International Association for Financial Planning (IAFP) and began his career as an independent financial advisor, specializing in tax-favored investing, retirement accumulation, and life insurance.

After building a successful practice as an independent advisor, Bill started helping other insurance and financial advisors build their own independent firms using the tools, strategies, and techniques he had found successful. Over the years, this became a very successful business helping independent financial advisors nationwide to properly advise their clients in retirement planning with life insurance and investments.

About ten years ago, Bill decided he wanted to reward his employees by sharing ownership in the company with them. He set out to create an employee stock ownership plan that would allow them to acquire lasting ownership in the company with no out-of-pocket cost and, therefore, no market risk to them.

The first part of the plan was straightforward—employee acquisition of stock:

- When employees reach their five year employment anniversary, they are given the opportunity to purchase shares of stock in the company with 100% financing at an extremely favorable loan rate.
- The valuation of the shares is based on a conservative formula, based on the company's revenue. As the company's revenue grows, so does the value of the shares.
- The interest rate on the loan is the lowest allowable by law, and there are no payments due for ten years from date of purchase.
- The collateral for the loan is limited to the shares of stock, themselves.
- Employees have all the rights of ownership of their stock, including the earnings of the company equal to their percentage of ownership.

The final part posed a challenge—ultimately empowering employees to own 100% of the company through a buy/sell agreement between Bill and the company.

The buy/sell agreement requires that 100% of the stock held by his estate, when he dies, would be sold to the company. The agreement would also require that the company buy the stock from the estate.

The question was: how to fund the purchase of such a large block of company stock?

One option would be to borrow the money, but that would burden the company with debt to borrow such a large amount.

Another option would be to start a sinking fund to save up enough money to fund the purchase of the shares. That option posed the same challenges as any other savings: Where do you put money that is liquid, has no market risk, and pays decent interest? And what to do when you do not know when you will need the entire lump sum? Bill would need enough life insurance to pay 70% of the value of the company to fund the buy/sell agreement at some unknown time in the future after his passing.

The solution? An IUL LASER Fund.

Bill took out a policy on himself, and as anticipated, funding that policy, with its massive tax advantages, has proven to be less expensive than the other options. In addition to providing enough money to fund the buy/sell agreement, the policy has allowed for access to money for emergencies as the years have gone by. And at the time of this writing, the employees own nearly 30% of the outstanding stock in the company. The original shares are worth nearly twice the original value, and the employees have received dividends every single year since the plan was set up.

With his buy/sell agreement, most people would say there was no need for Bill to buy any personal life insurance. His family would be well cared for with his sizable estate created from the large amount of cash generated by the sale of the company stock, as well as his other assets. But as a financial professional, Bill knew he could do even better for his family. Find out how Bill leveraged his assets to create a better approach to his estate plan—and had money when he needed it most—in the next chapter.

OUR OWN COMPANIES

We have taken advantage of The IUL LASER Fund as key person insurance. As the longtime face of the company, Doug's role as a national thought leader, bestselling author, YouTube and radio show host, and speaker has made him a central figure for the work we do. While Emron and Aaron and other members of the management team are taking on more of those roles, at this moment, if Doug were to suddenly pass away, the company would benefit from additional resources to continue the momentum (and of course, time to mourn the loss of Doug!).

For that reason, the company has taken out key person insurance on Doug. This gives the company and all of its employees the reassurance that there will be plenty of capital to continue work as usual and make plans for further growth.

BUILDING SECURITY

For more than thirty years, Henry Solomon has patiently built his real estate company from the ground up, literally. What started out as a business fixing up old homes has turned into a multimillion-dollar company owning and operating high density housing in an entire section of town. His net worth is upwards of $20 million. One of his sons works with him in the business, but Henry is largely the one running the show.

The company has taken out key person insurance on Henry to ensure that if Henry passes on, the company will have the capital necessary to continue. The insurance would also play a key role in maintaining family harmony should he pass on earlier than anticipated.

There are times when the head of a lucrative family business passes on, and the children not involved in the business may pressure those working with the family company to sell, so they can "get their share." In cases like this, the key person insurance helps protect the company, while a separate, personal IUL LASER Fund can provide for tax-free wealth transfer to posterity, keeping the lines clear and helping families avoid unnecessary rifts over money.

WIRED FOR BUSINESS PROTECTION

Bryant Minden is an orthodontist. Still in his thirties, he has established successful practices in two cities. He has IUL LASER Funds established that will serve as a special kind of buy-sell agreement, called a cross-purchase agreement. The difference is the policies are not in place with business partners. They're actually with competitors.

These orthodontists have amiably agreed to put agreements in place where should one of them pass away prematurely, they would use the policy to buy the other's practice, with the money going directly to the remaining spouse. This way it's a win-win for everyone. The orthodontists are able to have the funds to purchase the other's practice, while the deceased's spouse and families benefit from tax-free money.

Bryant and his wife also have a personal IUL LASER Fund to provide for income-tax-free death benefit and future retirement income. But by adding cross-purchase policies to the mix, he is able to secure added protection for his family should he pass away, and an opportunity to expand his business should one of the other orthodontists pass on.

WHAT CAN GO WRONG

As the owner of a busy print shop, Tom Paulson created an IUL LASER Fund to use as key person insurance in case he passed away prematurely. After a couple years of funding the policy, his print shop business started to decline. He figured it was just a down year, so he borrowed from his policy, tax-free, to cover expenses. As the business continued to spiral downward over the next few years, he continued to borrow from the policy. A few years later, he sold the company at a loss.

With a depleted IUL LASER Fund and no money to pay back the loans, he cancelled the policy. He expressed that he wished he had prioritized funding the policy or repaying at least part of the loans, because at least he would have been able to turn to his IUL LASER Fund for tax-free income after the loss of the business.

BEST LAID PLANS

Prudent business planning calls for mitigating all kinds of possible risks, but often the premature loss of a critical business leader is something businesses don't plan for. When managed properly, The IUL LASER Fund can help companies create valuable exit strategies—strategies that can not only help the business move forward, but also provide much-needed relief for those left behind.

8

Life's Emergencies

When the Olsons were in their 70s, they had set aside a good amount for retirement, mostly in taxed-as-earned accounts. After learning about The IUL LASER Fund, they started a series of strategic rollouts (as explained in Section I, Chapter 14) to move money from those accounts to an IUL LASER Fund. They wanted to diversify their portfolio and enjoy greater safety and tax-free advantages.

Over time, their initial $500,000 premium bucket accumulated a cash value of $1.6 million. For several years, the Olsons took out a modest $30,000 a year to supplement their retirement income (they have always been a frugal couple).

Now in their 90s, health challenges have necessitated their move to assisted and full-time care facilities. Their IUL LASER Fund has gone from providing retirement income, to serving as a robust emergency fund capable of covering the costs of the care they require.

For the Olson children, now raising their own children and grandchildren, their parents' IUL LASER Fund has been invaluable. Not only has the money made the best care possible for their parents, but it has also alleviated the otherwise significant financial burden they would be struggling to bear.

The Olsons simply borrow from their policy to pay for their costs each month. Because IUL LASER Fund loans do not have to be repaid during the life of the policy, the loan balance will simply be deducted from the death benefit when they pass away. In all, their IUL LASER Fund will have blessed their lives in many ways—from retirement income to an emergency fund, and finally an income-tax-free death benefit for their loved ones.

IN TIMES OF NEED

There's not one of us that hasn't experienced life's unpredictability. Whether it's an injury, an illness, a job loss, or a friend or loved one in need, The IUL LASER Fund can be a valuable reservoir, supplying the means to manage unexpected financial challenges.

The IUL LASER Fund's liquidity is key—with the ability to borrow money from the policy with an easy transfer, you're empowered to respond relatively quickly in times of need. Its tax advantages are also critical. With many other types of traditional vehicles, you may pay taxes and even penalties for early withdrawal when taking out money for an emergency. With The IUL LASER Fund, the money you borrow from the policy is tax-free.

And, as explained in Section I, Chapter 7, the money in your policy continues to grow even when you take out an Alternate Loan. Let's say your policy is averaging 7% interest, and you're being charged 5% interest on the loan. So between what your money is averaging, 7%, and what you're being charged for the loan, 5%, you're still averaging a 2% spread, depending on costs.

If you decide to never repay the loan, the balance simply goes against the death benefit upon your passing. If you choose to repay the loan, then your policy's cash value can grow even more. The IUL LASER Fund can give you peace of mind knowing that no matter how difficult life may get, your finances won't have to be difficult.

HELPING OTHERS

The Lees opened their IUL LASER Fund primarily for wealth transfer. Between good pensions and Social Security, they knew their retirement income would be covered. They wanted to put something in place that would ensure their children would receive a sizable inheritance upon their passing, income-tax-free.

They are in their 70s now, and they have been able to stick to their plan, relying on other sources of income for their retirement needs. There have been times, however, when they have dipped into their policy—times when they have been so glad to have it as a resource.

Over the years, some of their family members fell on hard times. As a tight-knit group, the Lees wanted to help, so they borrowed money from their policy to lend to loved ones. As those family members paid them back, they put the money right back into the policy.

Today their IUL LASER Fund is growing steadily, and they are grateful to have been in a position to help loved ones get through rough times.

EMERGENCY HOME REPAIRS

With their children grown and a while to go before retirement, the De-Witts were ready to get serious about planning for retirement. Working with their IUL specialist, they designed an IUL LASER Fund policy with a $200,000 premium bucket and began funding it with about $40,000 a year. After their fourth year of funding, they needed to do some emergency repairs on their home.

Rather than go through the hassle of qualifying for a home equity loan (with fees and required repayments), they turned to their IUL LASER Fund. They borrowed $60,000, tax-free—grateful for the liquidity and tax-advantaged access to the money when they needed it.

Once the repairs and renovation were complete, the DeWitts decided they would not repay the loan. It wasn't essential, and while it would impact the policy performance slightly, it was better for their budget to leave the policy about 70% funded.

Within a few years, they received an unexpected lump sum inheritance of $70,000. They wanted to put the money to work in a safe, tax-advantaged environment, and they were thrilled to have the perfect place for it—their IUL LASER Fund. They used the $70,000 to repay their policy loan. Today, their policy continues to grow, and they are looking forward to tax-free retirement income from The IUL LASER Fund, along with an income-tax-free death benefit for their family when they pass away.

ESTATE PLANNING TURNS TO LIFE-SAVING HEALTH CARE

In Section II, Chapter 7, we introduced Bill Zimmerman (his real name), a longtime financial professional who about ten years ago, utilized an IUL LASER Fund to fund a buy/sell agreement between his company and his employees. Having grown a successful business, Bill had also generated a high personal net worth. Between the value of his company, his real estate assets (a family home and a couple rental units), his brokerage account, IRA, 401(k), and cash, one might assume his estate plan was in a good place.

But Bill's financial education, training, and knowledge told him that his estate plan had two challenges. First, he understood the difference between theoretical paper losses and actual cash losses. With the major market corrections of 2000 to 2003 and 2008, he knew that even though stocks come back over the long run, the market can require a multiyear correction.

He knew that if you don't sell your stocks when the market is down, you have a theoretical paper loss, but you still have your shares. If you sell when the market is down, you realize an actual cash loss. This is why it is important to have at least three to six months' worth of cash for emergencies. It's also why if you're anticipating funding a big expenditure with money tied up in stocks, it's critical to liquidate those stocks well in advance. Otherwise, the market may drop when you have to sell, and you will be stuck realizing an actual cash loss.

Bill decided that he did not want to be subject to the whims and limitations of the market; he wanted to allocate $500,000 to a cash reserve account that could transfer to his family upon his passing.

He understood, however, that almost every traditional vehicle for cash reserves that are risk-free, liquid, and safe have their limitations: they pay little or no interest and are taxed as ordinary income. This is why Bill wanted an IUL LASER Fund.

He appreciated the safety of a 0% floor in the case of a downturn in the market, as well as the safety of working with reputable life insurance companies that have never defaulted on this type of account. He knew that the rate of return was likely to be reasonable, averaging around 7%, and he loved the tax-deferred growth. He liked knowing his policy provided liquidity, with money accessible in a few days with a simple phone call or transfer request. And he was relieved it could blossom and pass on to his family as an income-tax-free death benefit.

Now, Bill already had ample life insurance to provide funding for the buy/sell agreement in his employee stock program. It could be argued that he didn't need any more.

After considering all of his alternatives, Bill decided to purchase a relatively small policy, channeling that $500,000 into his IUL LASER Fund over the next five years. In it, he had liquidity, with money available for emergencies, earning a good rate of return, providing an eventual income-tax-free death benefit to his family, instead of going to the government in taxes.

A year and a half after he started this policy, Bill was diagnosed with stage 4 throat cancer and given a 50% chance of survival. He remembered it had a provision for critical illness: the policy could advance a percentage of the death benefit to help cover costs of a severe health crisis.

He had funded the policy with just $150,000 at this point, yet the company assured him he could collect $540,000 in advance, and still have a $400,000 policy with $40,000 in cash value. He used the money to provide for round-the-clock care, providing much-needed peace of mind for him and his wife to focus on his battle against the disease.

Talk about unintended consequences. All Bill wanted was a safe place to put some of his money he wanted to transfer to his family. What he got was a lot more by implementing an IUL LASER Fund.

As an update to Bill's story, he beat the cancer for a few years, while his IUL LASER Fund continued to grow tax-deferred. Sadly, he recently passed away due to complications from ALS. He passed on with the comfort of knowing he was able to transfer his money to his wife income-tax-free as a death benefit. We will miss you, Bill!

WHAT CAN GO WRONG

The Deans were a frugal couple in their 50s. With retirement around the corner, they opened a modest IUL LASER Fund with an $80,000 premium bucket, putting about $600 a month into the policy. About a year-and-a-half into their contribution phase, Paul Deans decided to make a change, pursuing a new career as a financial professional.

With the temporary cut he would take in pay as he built his new business, they needed emergency money to replace his income. They were about to borrow money from their policy tax-free, when Paul became enamored with the mutual funds he was starting to sell his clients. He was convinced he could do better by moving his money from his IUL LASER Fund into mutual funds, so the Deans decided to cancel their policy, pay the surrender charges, and transition their money into the at-risk, taxed-as-earned mutual fund.

A few years later, Paul mentioned that his job venture did not pan out, and now, even closer to retirement, they wished they had left their IUL LASER Fund in place. He expressed regret over pursuing a short-term gain rather than holding to financial discipline and a long-term perspective.

FOR ALL TYPES OF EMERGENCIES

Unfortunately the Deans missed out on what so many other families have benefited from—The IUL LASER Fund's flexibility and tax-free access to money. IUL LASER Funds are typically created for the income-tax-free death benefit, with additional objectives like retirement income or estate planning. But for many, when life's unseen setbacks strike, The IUL LASER Fund provides critical money for covering emergency expenses, providing for health care, and helping others.

9

Estate Planning

When Gerald and Jean Schwartz started their IUL LASER Fund, they did not have a lot of extra money to set aside. Their policy was structured so they could put in smaller amounts over a longer period of time, much like the "Starting at Age 40" example in Section I, Chapter 9.

Over the years, they dutifully socked away money whenever they could. What began as a modest policy grew to a significant amount of money over a few decades. As they neared retirement, Gerald and Jean began to do the things they had always dreamed of, borrowing money from their policy to travel and make memories with their children and grandchildren. They could not wait for retirement—they had so many things they wanted to do during their golden years.

Those years were cut short, however, when Jean suffered a heart attack. To honor his wife's legacy, Gerald used the death benefit from her passing to start another IUL LASER Fund. He structured this policy as part of a trust that called for equal opportunity versus equal distribution, outlining specific rules of governance for how Gerald's children and grandchildren could access the money for worthwhile pursuits like education and religious missions.

Gerald eventually married again, hoping to lessen the loneliness that had seeped in after Jean's passing. The family grew alarmed, however, when the second wife was frustrated that she could not get to the money in the trust. The second wife eventually moved on, leaving Gerald grateful that the trust, with its rules and guidelines in place, kept the money protected for his children and grandchildren. Gerald lived for a few more years, making the most of his time with his family.

Upon his passing, his children were surprised to learn they would receive more than $600,000 in an income-tax-free death benefit. Their humble parents had not only taught them valuable life lessons, but the Schwartz's financial discipline had blessed their posterity's lives through the family trust, and now again, through the gift of the death benefit.

PLANNING WISELY

As discussed in Section II, Chapter 1, there is a difference between traditional estate planning, which often relies on an equal distribution model, and the approach we recommend, an equal opportunity system. With equal distribution, while the parents are alive, the children and grandchildren often clamor for equal amounts of money, or cars, or vacations, doled out freely, without expectations or responsibility. And after the parents pass away, it's usually a simple formula: take the number of kids and divide that into the net worth, then divvy it out.

There are times when this calls for the successor trustee (often the oldest child) to liquidate assets in order to carve it all up. But this can be killing the goose laying the golden egg. If it's a family business or real estate holdings, suddenly the family is forced to sell it off—even if it may not be the best time to sell—just to satisfy the demands of the estate plans.

Instead, it can be more prudent to incorporate principles of equal opportunity into your estate planning. This way, while the parents are alive, the money in the family's Legacy Bank—in an IUL LASER Fund policy, for example—is available to those who comply with the family's rules of governance.

Say, for example, you had an IUL LASER Fund from which your grandchildren could borrow money for education. That "equal opportunity" would be there for all of your grandchildren. But it's not without accountability and responsibility. Your rules of governance may require them to save half of their tuition, which you would match with money from your IUL LASER Fund. Or it may call for the loan to be repaid back into the policy, at a nominal interest rate.

Upon your passing, your Equal Opportunity Trust may require family members receiving part of your income-tax-free death benefit to meet certain requirements, or use part of the money to open another IUL LASER Fund policy for their own children and grandchildren. This way you can perpetuate the family's Legacy Bank and Values & Vision for generations to come.

However it's structured and utilized, The IUL LASER Fund can be a valuable, flexible part of your estate planning.

TAX-ADVANTAGED PLANNING

Stan McDowell is in his early 60s, actively engaged in his career, the community, and family life. Having planned well for the future, he has several financial strategies in place that will provide for a comfortable retirement in the next few years.

A few years ago, Stan wanted to explore his estate planning options, with the goal to set aside money that he would not touch during retirement—he wanted it exclusively for wealth transfer to his kids when he passes away. After looking at a number of strategies, he opened an IUL LASER Fund. He liked the tax-deferred growth, the safety from losses due to downturns in the market, and above all, the income-tax-free death benefit.

He created a policy with a $300,000 premium bucket, which currently would provide more than $700,000 in income-tax-free death benefit for his family should he pass away prematurely. If he lives to age 85 or more (which with his good health and life expectancy he should), his family will receive more than $1 million in income-tax-free death benefit. That is considerably more than they would have received if he had put it in a traditional account, and he is grateful to have found a solution that can blossom in value and bless his family when he is no longer around to provide for them himself.

WELL-BEING FOR THE ENTIRE FAMILY

The Romanos had built a health and wellness practice for over forty years and were getting ready to retire when they learned about The IUL LASER Fund. Over the next five years, they created a total of four policies, repositioning assets that had been in traditional low-interest savings accounts, IRAs and 401(k)s. They were glad to see this money now safe, liquid, growing tax-deferred with predictable rates of return, and positioned to transfer to their children income-tax-free upon their passing.

In the years since, their policies have grown enough that they could currently take as much as $200,000 in tax-free retirement income if they chose to. They do have other sources of income, though, so they are content to let their policies continue to grow for an eventual wealth transfer. Since their death benefits are already double the amount they originally put into their IUL LASER Funds, this has proven an optimal estate planning strategy for the Romanos.

Based on the principles discussed in Section II, Chapter I, in addition to cash, the Romanos are also intent on transferring their KASH to their posterity. They have created a KASH Blueprint, which has guided the establishment of their Equal Opportunity Trust, a revocable living trust with rules of governance for equal opportunity, rather than equal distribution.

Now their children and grandchildren have specific parameters to ensure that those who want to access the money in their family's Legacy Bank will be able to do so for things like college, religious and humanitarian missions, weddings, business ventures, and more.

By utilizing The IUL LASER Fund, outlining their KASH Blueprint, and establishing an Equal Opportunity Trust, the Romanos will pass along far more, in every aspect of life, than they ever thought possible.

WHAT CAN GO WRONG

With more than $15 million in net worth, the Ramseys were confident in their financial future. They had never considered acquiring life insurance, as they assumed their sizable estate would be more than enough to transfer their wealth to their children. That was, however, until they learned more about estate taxes.

At the time, estate taxes for estates valued at over $675,000 ranged from 37% to 55%—due within nine months of the second parent's passing. When they considered the impact that would have on their family—likely necessitating the liquidation of $6 million in assets to cover 55% in estate taxes—they decided a policy that could cover the eventual cost of estate taxes might be a good idea after all.

They designed a $6 million second-to-die policy that they would minimum fund—this policy was created to cover the eventual cost of the estate taxes. They also opened an IUL LASER Fund with a $3 million death benefit on Rex and another with a $2 million death benefit on Nancy. They planned on maximum funding these policies, looking forward not only to the income-tax-free death benefit these policies would pass on to their children, but also the safety and tax-deferred growth.

Within a couple years, Nancy contracted a terminal illness. With a shorter life expectancy, the Ramseys adjusted her policy to minimum fund it, so it could provide the most death benefit in the shortest amount of time possible. Nancy passed away, and her $2 million income-tax-free death benefit passed on to her children. (Rex had named them the beneficiaries, as he did not need the money.) Within two years, the children had squandered that $2 million death benefit. They assumed it would not be a problem—their family estate had plenty more where that came from.

Rex soon experienced health complications himself. He named one of his sons successor trustee so he could step back from the day-to-day management of the estate. That son let the $6 million policy designed to cover estate taxes lapse. He also let his father's IUL LASER Fund lapse. When Rex passed away unexpectedly from an accident, the children found themselves with no death benefit to help them pay for estate taxes, let alone receive the inheritance they had anticipated.

A PRUDENT PLAN

When funded and structured properly, The IUL LASER Fund can provide the means for an income-tax-free transfer of your estate's wealth to your children and grandchildren. When combined with a KASH Blueprint and Rules of Governance, it can also become a generator for future generations to successfully perpetuate your family's legacy of Authentic Wealth.

10

Real Estate

The Meachams had long believed in IRAs and 401(k)s. That is, until 2008 when they nearly lost everything in their traditional accounts. They were frustrated and did not know what else to do for retirement. They learned about The IUL LASER Fund, but were skeptical—didn't everyone say insurance isn't the answer?

They investigated the strategies further and decided to give The IUL LASER Fund a try. Over the next six years, they maximum funded their policy and then did something they never thought possible: bought a retirement home for cash. They borrowed the money from their policy and paid for it, completely.

They decided they would rather act as their own bank than give interest to yet another institution. So the Meachams are paying "themselves" back, making regular loan payments to the policy faithfully just as they would a mortgage company. In a couple years when they have paid off that loan, they will begin to take retirement income from their IUL LASER Fund.

Coming off the losses of 2008, they marvel at the difference in how they feel: safe from the whims of the market, confident and in control of their future. They are grateful they dared to take a look at insurance, because it empowered them to make real estate decisions they could not have otherwise. And as they look ahead to retirement, they realize insurance is an effective answer.

REAL ESTATE STRATEGIES

Real estate is a core part of many Americans' financial portfolios. Whether it's a condo, a large home, or a string of commercial properties, most of us have ownership of some type of real estate.

However, as a financial vehicle, real estate can be fickle. It can provide equity and security during good economic times, but it can also prove to be a liability and loss when the market turns south.

By combining The IUL LASER Fund with prudent real estate strategies, however, many of those liabilities can be mitigated, and really profound things can happen.

GETTING REAL

Spacious, in a picturesque location, the Russells loved their home. They had raised their family there and planned on staying in the home as they approached retirement. As we met with them, we helped them reframe how they saw the value of their house. Now that they were empty nesters, they did not need such a large house. If they downsized, they would have even more money to set aside for retirement.

They caught on to the idea, realizing if they sold their home for a $600,000 profit, they could turn around, buy a smaller retirement home for $300,000 and put the other $300,000 into an IUL LASER Fund, where it could compound safely, with liquidity, predictable rates of return, and tax advantages just waiting for them in retirement. They one-upped the original plan, deciding instead to pay just $50,000 down on their retirement home so they could set aside another $250,000 into their IUL LASER Fund.

They sold their big home, bought a beautiful retirement home, and transferred the money into their IUL LASER Fund over the next five years.

Now, they have more than enough to make the mortgage payments (the mortgage is 4.5%, and their IUL LASER Fund has been earning 7% to 10% over the past few years). In fewer than ten years, their policy has now grown to the point where they are about $200,000 ahead of where they would have been had they paid cash for their new house and invested just the $300,000 net equity out of their sale. The Russells successfully leveraged real estate to create an IUL LASER Fund that will not only provide a valuable income-tax-free death benefit for their children and grandchildren someday, but that will also provide retirement income throughout their golden years.

LOCATION, LOCATION, LOCATION

When the Heaths first moved to their home in Northern California, it was in a lovely, middle-class area. Over the years they added to the home, made some renovations, and enjoyed raising their family in the growing community. With several children and plenty of expenses, however, they had not been able to set aside much for retirement.

By the time the kids had grown—many of them living in other states— they wondered if it wouldn't be a good idea to sell their home. Their area had become one of the most sought-after locations in California, with home values skyrocketing. But they hesitated over capital gains taxes. Would it just be better to sit on the house and try to figure out a Plan B for retirement?

Then they did the math, which was enough to convince them. They sold their home for $4.3 million and paid capital gains taxes of just over $1 million. They built a large, beautiful home near children and grandchildren and had $2.4 million left to set aside.

By the time The IUL LASER Fund is maximum-funded and they begin taking retirement income, they will be able to take about $200,000 a year, tax-free. On top of it all, when the Heaths pass away, their children will receive a sizable income-tax-free death benefit. They cannot believe the difference it made for their retirement to combine the power of real estate and The IUL LASER Fund.

CLOSING THE GAP

The Sheltons could have found themselves in a bind. They were about to close on their new home, one they had fallen in love with and planned to retire in within the next ten years or so, but their current house was still in escrow. With at least a month's gap between the closings on the two homes, they would have been at risk of forfeiting the purchase of the new house.

Fortunately, the Sheltons had two IUL LASER Funds they could turn to—one with a $450,000 premium bucket, and the other with about a $200,000 premium bucket. They borrowed from both policies and used that tax-free access to completely pay for their new house, in cash.

About a month after moving in, the sale of their previous home was finalized, and they put the money from the sale of that home right back into their policies to repay the loans.

Today, they are living in their retirement home which they own with no mortgage, and their policies continue to grow. In a few years, they'll begin to take tax-free retirement income from their IUL LASER Funds, and enjoy financial peace of mind during their golden years.

LANDING A GOOD DEAL

Alicia Derrick was selling an office building she owned, implementing a reverse 1031 exchange (which provides unique tax advantages). She was also poised to buy a parcel of land, the purchase of which was urgent. Rather than stress about trying to get financing in a relatively short amount of time, she borrowed money from her IUL LASER Funds to cover the purchase of the land.

She had $1.3 million between her two IUL LASER Funds. She took out a total of about $400,000, tax-free, bought the land right away, and now she has the luxury of time to sell the office building in the coming months.

While she does not have to, Alicia is planning to repay the loans with money she gets from the sale of the office building. She has several years before retirement, during which time her policies can accumulate even more value. Eventually she plans on taking tax-free retirement income from her policies, and in the meantime, she is grateful for the flexibility her IUL LASER Funds have given her to manage her real estate investments. Imagine if her money were in a highly appreciated stock, she would never sell the stock to buy the property because she would pay significant capital gains. Or if her money were in IRAs or 401(k)s, she would never take out that much money in one year because of loan limits and taxes. Her IUL LASER Fund is extremely flexible, and gave her the ability to get the money when she needed it.

CHANGING THEIR FUTURE

The Heatons owned a small business, working hard every day to provide for their family. With an eye toward the future, they were disciplined savers. With safety as a priority, they were leery of losing money in the stock market, so they had been setting aside money largely in traditional bank accounts, earning very modest interest.

They worried, though. Between their savings and Social Security, they would not have enough during retirement to make ends meet. In the short-term, if Zach Heaton were to die prematurely, the family business would likely not survive. They wanted to find a better way to secure their financial situation now—and down the road.

One of their greatest assets was a piece of real estate, but they knew the property risked losing value if the real estate market turned. They decided to reposition and transfer the value of the bank accounts and the real estate from one asset class to another, and they opened an IUL LASER Fund. Sure enough, the market did drop in their area, and they were grateful they had taken action, otherwise they would have lost the value of the property.

Now, over a decade later, their IUL LASER Fund has over $1 million in cash value. Their money continues to grow tax-deferred in the policy, and they have the reassurance of an income-tax-free death benefit of over $2 million. When they retire, they will be able to access annual tax-free income of over $78,000. If they had left their money in their traditional accounts, it would have yielded just over $15,000 in annual retirement income. Things look much brighter for the Heatons, and they love the peace of mind that brings.

WHAT CAN GO WRONG

As mentioned throughout this book, financial self-discipline is critical for IUL LASER Fund success. The lack of that self-discipline can prove counterproductive, as in this example of a client who wanted to use The IUL LASER Fund for real estate purposes.

The Hafens had been contemplating making extra payments to the mortgage company to pay off their home within fifteen years. They decided, instead, to put those dollars into their IUL LASER Fund to maximum fund their policy sooner (in five years rather than the seven or eight they had been planning).

This way those extra dollars could go to work earning tax-deferred interest in the policy, rather than just paying down a mortgage. They liked the idea of eventually having enough to pay off their mortgage if they chose to borrow it out of the policy, but thinking they would likely leave the money in their policy where it would be liquid, safe from downturns in the real estate market, and able to continue earning a rate of return.

Things were moving along, with the extra payments they were funneling into their IUL LASER Fund on target to have enough to pay off their mortgage in twelve years (setting aside the same amount that a fifteen-year mortgage would require). Then they decided to take some money out for a family vacation with the kids. Then they decided to purchase an RV, so they pulled more money from their policy. While they were at it, they decided to scoop a large chunk of money out to finish the basement of their home.

Within fifteen years, they were frustrated they did not meet their goal of having enough money in their policy to pay off their mortgage—and their policy was still not maximum-funded. They had depleted their policy to consume, rather than funding their policy to save. They ended up cashing out what was left in their policy. Treating their policy like an ATM not only led to disappointment, but it also robbed them of The IUL LASER Fund's liquidity, safety, rate of return, and tax advantages that could have helped sustain them throughout their retirement years.

BRINGING IT HOME

When looking at retirement, you can blend real estate and The IUL LASER Fund in multiple ways to make the most of your future. If you're looking to downsize, selling valuable real estate can provide the means to set aside a good amount of money for retirement—money that might not otherwise be available in your financial situation. Conversely, if your IUL LASER Fund has enough value, you can leverage its liquidity to take out a loan and purchase real estate outright. However you approach it, combining strategies can give you more momentum toward a brighter future.

11

Strategic Rollouts

The time had come. George Witt was at the age when he would have to begin taking Required Minimum Distributions on his IRAs or face IRS penalties. But he did not need the retirement income yet. And he did not like the look of how taxes would take a toll on those minimum withdrawals. He was worried this approach would eventually drain his nest egg, perhaps before he passed on.

He had already survived one of the worst decades in America's financial history, where his IRAs suffered big losses, twice. In 2000 he had $600,000 in his traditional accounts. By 2010, his battle-worn accounts were just barely recovering, returning to the original $600,000 balance. He wanted safety. And he wanted better tax advantages.

George decided to do a strategic rollout, get his taxes over and done with, and transition his money into an IUL LASER Fund that could provide greater safety, predictable rates of return, and tax-free income.

Over the next five years, he pulled $150,000 a year from his IRA, paid taxes, and moved it to an IUL LASER Fund. By the end of those five years, he had paid all of his taxes and maximum funded his policy. His money was now safe from the volatility of the market. He was enjoying predictable rates of return of 7% to 10%. He could take an annual tax-free income of more than $50,000 from his policy—which was over three times the $16,000 he would have been taking in after-tax annual income from his IRA.

George's financial portfolio was now providing so much more than he needed that he was able to create a family Legacy Bank, which his children and grandchildren could access for endeavors like school, weddings, and business ventures. In addition to it all, he now had an income-tax-free way to transfer his wealth to his children through The IUL LASER Fund's death benefit.

THE ADVANTAGE OF STRATEGIC ROLLOUTS

As mentioned in Section I, taxes are a necessary part of a thriving democracy. We're proponents of everyone paying their fair share. But we're not advocates of paying more than is necessary, and it has been argued that IRAs and 401(k)s were set up with Uncle Sam's blessing for a reason. From penalties on early withdrawals to RMDs and penalties for late withdrawal, the IRS can get exactly what it wants from these traditional accounts.

That said, IRAs and 401(k)s can have a worthwhile place in your financial portfolio. It is simply wise to look at times when it's prudent to move money from traditional accounts and into an IUL LASER Fund.

This empowers you to get your taxes over and done with on money in those accounts, especially if you have room in your current marginal tax bracket. To illustrate, let's say you're married filing jointly, and your taxable income this year is $325,000. According to current tax rates, you're in a marginal tax bracket of 32%. Let's say you want to move money from your 401(k) to an IUL LASER Fund in a strategic rollout. The next marginal tax bracket starts at $400,001, so you essentially have "room" to move $75,000 out of your 401(k) and still remain in your marginal tax bracket of 32%.

Getting taxes over and done with could be compared to pre-paid legal, where you're paying in advance for something impending down the road. You're essentially pre-paying taxes in a bracket that you will probably never see lower again in the future.

As discussed in Section I, Chapter 14, when that is the case, strategic rollouts can provide an effective means to get taxes over and done with, and to reposition part or all of your money in vehicles like The IUL LASER Fund that can provide greater liquidity, safety, predictable rates of return, and tax advantages.

ROLLIN' ON

Their IRAs were burgeoning. By the time the Moores were ready to retire, everything they had set aside, from pensions to 401(k)s and IRAs, had rolled over into overstuffed IRAs with over $4 million in their tax-deferred accounts. They were in the highest tax bracket, and the thought of eventually taking RMDs of about $200,000 a year and getting hit with about 40% in taxes felt like a painful way to access retirement income.

They learned about The IUL LASER Fund from a family member who had enjoyed all the liquidity, safety, predictable rates of return, and tax advantages, and they wanted to consider their options. They decided to do a strategic rollout, get the taxes over with, and move their money where they could get better safety and tax-free access.

They are in the process now of transitioning that money, and in another five years or so they will have maximum funded a couple policies. In all, they will save over $1 million in taxes using this strategy rather than keeping their money in the IRAs and withdrawing RMDs.

Their money is growing tax-deferred in the policy. They will be able to take tax-free retirement income from their IUL LASER Fund—several hundred thousand dollars a year if they would like. And when they pass away, their children will receive a multimillion-dollar income-tax-free death benefit.

ESCAPING THE TAX TRAP

The Barlows had been saving for retirement religiously, tucking away the maximum amount each year in Ray's IRAs and Sarah's 401(k). They

were looking forward to reaping the rewards of their financial dili-
gence—until they realized how much Uncle Sam was looking forward
to it, as well.

Upon closer analysis, they discovered if they continued making annual maximum contributions to their IRAs and 401(k), they would accrue
about $750,000 in their tax-deferred accounts by the time they retired.
When they eventually took withdrawals, they would likely pay at least
a third of that in taxes, or about $250,000. If they buckled down and
strung out their withdrawals, taking RMDs to their full life expectancy,
their at-retirement tax bill could rise as high as half a million dollars.

The Barlows wanted to step away, far away, from the jaws of that tax
trap and reduce their at-retirement tax bill. (The concept of the at-retirement tax bill is one we introduced in Section I, Chapter 2—making
sure you put yourself in as favorable a tax situation as possible during
retirement. You want to avoid being stuck with a majority of tax-deferred financial vehicles that can take a toll on your income during retirement.)

They performed a strategic rollout over the next seven years, repositioning their money from their IRAs and 401(k) into two IUL LASER
Funds and getting their taxes on that money over and done with. They
simultaneously executed tax-saving strategies to mitigate their overall
tax bill.

For the past twenty years now, their IUL LASER Funds have been growing protected from downturns in the market, earning superior rates of
return. They are looking at tax-free retirement income that is far greater than what they would have had with their taxed-on-the-harvest traditional accounts. They also have an income-tax-free way to transfer
wealth to their children with the death benefit on their policies. This
approach has created a more abundant future than they could have ever
imagined.

WHAT CAN GO WRONG

With about five years to go before retirement, the Kramers wanted to
minimize their at-retirement tax bill. They began a strategic rollout,

getting their taxes over and done with and moving their money from their IRAs and 401(k)s to an IUL LASER Fund.

Five years later, their policy was fully funded, and they began to take tax-free retirement income. Everything was humming along until they talked with a financial advisor who was not familiar with The IUL LASER Fund. He convinced them they were missing out, not having their money in the market.

They decided to cancel their policy and move their money into a variable annuity. This was at the beginning of 2008. By the end of that year, their annuity had lost 40% of its value. Their son, who has an IUL LASER Fund, has shared that the Kramers have regretted their decision ever since, watching his policy grow tax-deferred steadily and safely, protected from losses due to downturns in the market.

YOUR FUTURE, NOT UNCLE SAM'S

Strategic rollouts are an effective way to diversify your **at-retirement** income. You are deciding when to get the taxes over with, and you are deciding to position your money in an IUL LASER Fund where you can enjoy tax-free retirement income and an income-tax-free death benefit for your beneficiaries. You are also putting your money where the market can't hurt it. Indexing protects your money from losses due to volatility in the market, and predictable rates of return can give you the reassurance of gauging how much growth you can expect, on average. These knowns can provide greater peace of mind as you approach your future.

12

Tax Reduction

They had just turned age 60 when they started to seriously analyze their retirement plans. The Garners had spent their careers working hard, earning a moderate income. They anticipated they would have enough for retirement between their pensions and other tradition-al accounts (including 401[k]s, 403[b]s, and TSAs—with a total value of $250,000). They had just rolled these supplemental accounts over into an IRA, and were wondering whether they should begin withdrawing money from the IRA during their 60s, or wait until later. At the advice of an accountant, they were leaning toward waiting until their 70s, thus deferring and delaying the inevitable tax. They met with us to look more closely at overall, long-term tax-minimization strategies and immedi-ately saw the fallacy in continued tax-deferral.

If they waited until they had to start taking RMDs, they could end up sending as much as $250,000 in taxes to Uncle Sam over the course of their retirement years (because they would be "stretching the IRA out" to their life expectancy). This was shocking, as they only had $250,000 total in their IRA at the time. They couldn't afford to give Uncle Sam that much—and they wanted a better quality of life for themselves.

They ended up deciding to do a strategic rollout. Over the next five years, they moved their money from their IRAs, got their taxes over with, and transferred their money into an IUL LASER Fund. By doing so, they ended up paying about $60,000 in total taxes on that $250,000—which is over four times less than they would have if they had kept their money in the IRAs.

Now their money continues to grow in their IUL LASER Fund, where it is safe from downturns in the market and can provide tax-free retirement income from this point forward.

TAX REDUCTION

One of the best ways to make the most out of retirement income is make sure *you* get the most out of your retirement income, rather than Uncle Sam. That's why tax reduction tends to be one of the primary reasons people choose IUL LASER Funds.

If you're putting money into an IUL LASER Fund that has already been taxed (such as from regular income, a money market, savings account, the sale of a property, etc.), once inside your IUL LASER Fund, your money can grow tax-deferred, and you can access it tax-free and transfer it income-tax-free to your heirs upon your passing.

If you're looking to put money into your IUL LASER Fund from tax-deferred accounts, you will likely want to do a strategic rollout (see more on strategic rollouts in Section I, Chapter 14 and Section II, Chapter 11). This way you can minimize the impact of taxes—and adhere to TAMRA—while you transition your money into an IUL LASER Fund.

Now keep in mind, it's not imperative to move every cent you have in tax-deferred accounts to an IUL LASER Fund. As we discussed in Section I, Chapter 2, it is just as important to diversify your "tax portfolio" as it is to diversify your financial portfolio. Depending on age, tax brackets, health, and other factors, there may be compelling reasons to keep part or all of your money in tax-deferred accounts. If so, there may be options for how to manage the money within those accounts that can give you better liquidity, safety, predictable rates of return, and tax advantages. It's important to work with an experienced financial professional to weigh all of your options and choose solutions that are best for you.

FROM HIGH TO LOW

Steve and Leslie Franks had been in the highest tax bracket for years. Now in their 60s, they were looking ahead, and the last thing they wanted to do was split their future retirement income with Uncle Sam any more than they had to. Having suffered the ravages of the Great Recession, they were also eager to enjoy better predictability without market risk—and they wanted to ensure their money would pass on income-tax-free to their children through a death benefit.

They made a plan for a strategic rollout, taking into account their unique tax implications. At the time, they were living in a state that did not have state income tax—but they were planning on eventually moving to a state that would have exorbitant state income taxes. Furthermore, federal tax brackets were set to increase soon. The resulting strategic rollout was aggressive, moving as much as nearly $2 million from traditional accounts and paying over $600,000 in taxes in a single year. While that may sound high, this strategy provided for considerable tax savings as compared to if they had waited to pay taxes.

In the end, they transitioned their money into four IUL LASER Fund policies—two for Steve and two for Leslie—putting a total of $4 million into the policies. To further diversify their portfolios, they worked with two different insurance companies and chose different indexing strategies for each policy.

Fast forward ten years, and their money in their policies has grown to over $7 million. Because their taxes are over and done with, as they start to take retirement income now (just under $200,000 a year), they are doing so tax-free. With their tax-free income and tax deductions, they are effectively in a 0% tax bracket now.

Going from paying the most in taxes to the least, the Franks are grateful to be looking forward to an abundant retirement, one where taxes can no longer impact their income, and where their heirs will receive an inheritance income-tax-free, through the death benefit on their policies.

THAT'S ENOUGH, UNCLE SAM

With just a few years left before retirement, Jim Woodrow had a diverse retirement portfolio awaiting him. But there was something nagging at him—one of his retirement accounts was an IRA, with $100,000. While he would not necessarily need that IRA for primary retirement income, he also did not want to pay more in taxes than necessary.

He decided to do a strategic rollout over the next five years, getting the taxes over with, and maximum funding an IUL LASER Fund.

He has since finished the rollout, and his policy has been earning nearly 8% interest per year. He has just started taking out a nominal amount, tax-free, to supplement his retirement income—about $10,000 a year. He is relieved to have the taxes over with, and glad to add that $100,000 going to work in a tax-deferred environment, providing tax-free supplemental income, with the opportunity to pass along a death benefit to his heirs.

A CPA – CONVINCED OF A BETTER PATH

As a CPA, Sydney Weston is meticulous about her finances. When she heard about The IUL LASER Fund through a professional networking group, she, like many people learning about these strategies for the first time, was impressed ... but hesitant. She wondered if it could really provide benefits that IRAs and 401(k)s could not.

She examined details like IRS codes 7702 and 72(e). She explored the safety of entrusting her money to 100-year-plus insurance institutions and a 0% floor during market downturns. She weighed the living benefits, such as tax-free retirement income.

Her thorough analysis did not stop there. She enlisted the keen eyes of colleagues, including a chartered financial professional and tax attorney. These professionals confirmed that the IRS codes were employed to create exactly the tax-free retirement income that had been suggested; that the IRS codes 7702 and 72(e) would in fact give her tax-free benefits for life; and that the structured format of The IUL LASER Fund could provide the safe, cost-effective, and tax-advantaged solution she was looking for.

She opened an IUL LASER Fund, and now enjoys the confidence of tax-free income—even to age 100 and beyond—and an income-tax-free death benefit for her heirs when she passes on.

THE ARTISTRY OF PRUDENT PLANNING

With a successful career as self-employed entrepreneurs in the arts, the Carters realized they needed to get serious about setting money aside for retirement. They veered away from IRAs and chose an IUL LASER Fund, because they understood the value of paying taxes on the seed rather than the harvest.

They put about $3,000 a month into their policy to maximum fund their policy, but they wanted to do more. They sold their large home and downsized to a beautiful retirement community, then used the $300,000 from the sale of their home (which was capital-gains-tax-free) to create a second IUL LASER Fund.

Over the past ten years, their IUL LASER Funds have given them greater financial flexibility to pursue their other passions, including serving religious and humanitarian missions and traveling to visit their children and grandchildren. They pay taxes only on their earned income from their art business, and the rest—about $30,000 a year—is tax-free income from their IUL LASER Funds. Like many of our clients, they are enjoying a life-style that is more than double what is reflected in earned income on their tax returns—which is in perfect compliance with tax codes.

Not only are they enjoying a more abundant life now, but they have the reassurance of knowing they will pass along that abundance to their children upon their passing, through the income-tax-free death benefit on their policies.

WHAT CAN GO WRONG

The Smiths had $450,000 in taxed-as-earned accounts, and they were tired of getting hammered on taxes. As soon as they learned about The IUL LASER Fund's tax-deferred growth, tax-free access to money, and income-tax-free death benefit, they were ready for a brighter tax future.

They repositioned their money and were enjoying the tax-deferred growth for several years when they met with a financial advisor who was not well-versed in IUL LASER Funds. He insisted they would do better by pulling their money out and allowing him to put it to work in the market.

We cautioned them—canceling the policy would trigger a tax event on the money their policy had gained over the years. Their policy had been averaging about a 9% annual rate of return, and its cash value was now over $900,000. They were determined, however, and followed through with their plan. They were shocked when April 15 rolled around and they had to pay taxes on the growth—totaling about $150,000 in taxes.

If they had left their money in the policy, it could have continued to grow tax-deferred, provided tax-free access to money, and income-tax-free transfer of wealth to their children through the death benefit. Instead of a tax reduction, they experienced tax devastation.

MAXIMIZING YOUR FUTURE

While paying taxes is an important responsibility for all of us as Americans, by utilizing proven strategies, it is possible to get necessary taxes over and done with, and avoid paying unnecessary taxes. With The IUL LASER Fund's tax advantages, you can give yourself the ultimate advantage during retirement—tax-free retirement income and income-tax-free wealth transfer to your heirs.

You can also enjoy greater liquidity, safety, and predictable rates of returns that can empower you to bring opportunities to your children and grandchildren, to give more to charity, and to pursue personal pastimes.

In all, whether your goals include accessing working capital, managing risk in business planning, protecting yourself with emergency funds, or reducing your taxes, The IUL LASER Fund's versatility can help you maximize your future in multiple ways. In addition, The IUL LASER Fund's income-tax-free death benefit provides a way to transfer your wealth to future generations.

As you combine these strategies for the Financial Dimension with tactics for your Intellectual and Foundational Dimensions (mentioned in Section II, Chapter 1), you can leave a lasting legacy for Authentic Wealth to future generations. We wish you all the best as you move forward, toward a brighter, more abundant future.

Flip to Read Section I

TOP 5 TAKEAWAYS

1. Owning an IUL LASER Fund is essentially self-insuring your own death benefit.

2. In the early days of Universal Life (in the early 1980s), when the policy was maximum-funded, the insurance company was no longer at risk for the death benefit.

3. When the government passed TEFRA/DEFRA, it redefined insurance as "risk management," and mandated a corridor between what a policyholder put in, and the death benefit, based on factors like age, gender, and health.

4. The advantage of this to you, the policyholder, is now you know exactly how much money you're going to put in the policy, because you're the one who determines your IUL LASER Fund's Guideline Single Premium.

5. By complying with TEFRA/DEFRA, you can reap all the potential rewards of liquidity, safety, rates of return, and tax advantages with your properly structured, maximum-funded IUL policy.

14

Staying Balanced

Take a look at a recipe, something fundamentally delicious, like classic Nestlé ® Toll House® Cookies:

> 2¼ cups all-purpose flour
> 1 teaspoon baking soda
> 1 teaspoon salt
> 1 cup (2 sticks) butter, softened
> ³/4 cup granulated sugar
> ³/4 cup packed brown sugar
> 1 teaspoon vanilla extract
> 2 large eggs
> 2 cups (12-oz. pkg.) NESTLÉ® TOLL HOUSE® Semi-Sweet
>   Chocolate Morsels
> 1 cup chopped nuts

Blended well, crisped to crunchy perfection on the outside and melty cocoa on the inside ... there's nothing quite like a cookie right out of the oven. But what if we changed things up?

What if we took the sugars down to ¼ cup each, doubled the butter, and tripled the salt? What emerges from the oven would be salty, chocolate-speckled sludge. Without a good balance of ingredients, even cookies can go from just-right to all-wrong.

Balance is critical in most things—from our work-and-family lives to the construction of our city's soaring skyscrapers. It's also critical in your financial approach, where it's wise to use a blend of strategies so that all of your eggs (or nest eggs) aren't in one basket.

HOW MUCH INSURANCE?

Clearly, we recommend that an IUL LASER Fund be an integral part of your overall financial portfolio. The liquidity, safety, predictable rates of return, and tax advantages are something you don't want to pass up. So just how much insurance should you get?

The better question to start with is how much insurance CAN you get?

When it comes to life insurance, nothing is a given. You need to qualify in essentially three areas:

1. You must undergo a medical exam.
2. You must adhere to affordability guidelines, as outlined by your insurance company.
3. You must demonstrate a need for the death benefit for reasons that may include income replacement, estate preservation, wealth transfer, retirement income, etc.

HEALTH STATUS

Like all life insurance, most looking to initiate an IUL LASER Fund policy will receive what's called a health rating. Since the amount of insurance required under TEFRA and DEFRA is based upon your age, your gender, and your health, your health rating plays a role in your policy.

Some people may need to undergo a medical exam to receive their health rating. If you have had some health issues—do not count yourself out. We have had several clients with chronic diseases or other health challenges who have been able to open IUL LASER Funds. There are strategies your IUL specialist can help you with, such as "squeezing down" the death benefit, that can make policies effective.

AFFORDABILITY GUIDELINES

Insurance companies use affordability guidelines to ensure premium payments are aligned with the policyholders' financial ability, including income, net worth, and liquidity. In this regard, they're acting as a fiduciary on your behalf to make sure that you're not allocating more to an insurance policy than you have resources for.

Generally, the higher the net worth or income, the larger the percentage of that income or net worth can be put toward an insurance policy. This approach is designed to help individuals avoid overextending themselves. Here's a quick snapshot in Figure 14.1, of general guidelines (which are subject to change—your IUL specialist can provide the latest figures; while every insurance company has different guidelines, the following numbers are provided below as an example from one particular insurance company):

FIGURE 14.1

For Premium Payments from Income				
Income	<=$75,000	$75,001-$149,999	$150,000-$199,999	$200,000+
Maxium Total Planned Allowed	10%-20% (plus minimum premium requirement)	15%-30%	25%-40%	Underwriter Discretion

As you can see, if your income is less than or equal to $75,000, this insurance company will allow only 10% to 20% of that income to be the premium, or up to $7,500 to $15,000 a year. If your income is $75,001 to $149,999, then 15% to 30% of your income would be allowed for premiums, or about $11,250 to $44,700 a year. If your income is between $150,000 and $199,000, you would be looking at 25% to 40% of your income, or $37,500 to $79,600. And if $200,000 or above, the percentage would be up to the underwriter. It wouldn't be unusual if you're making $500,000 a year for the underwriter to judge you as financially savvy, and allow up to 50% your income, or $250,000 a year, in premiums.

FIGURE 14.2

For Premium Payments from Net Worth (calculated on net worth, applied to liquid assets)				
Net Worth	<=$500,000	$500,001-$1,499,999	$1,500,000-$1,999,999	$2,000,000+
Percentage of Liquid Assets Allowed for Total Planned Premium	20%	30%	40%	Underwriter Discretion

Now if your affordability is going to be based on net worth, the insurance company will look at your liquid assets (see Figure 14.2). Liquid assets would include investments, brokerage accounts, savings accounts, IRAs, 401(k)s—anything you can get cash out of (but not assets such as real estate equity or personal property). So if your net worth is $500,000 but your liquid assets are, say, $100,000, you would only be allowed 20% of that $100,000, or $20,000 a year, in premiums. You can see in this chart that your percentages go up to 30% and 40% of your liquid assets, based on net worth. After $2 million, the underwriter will make the call. The underwriter may say, "This policyholder is worth $10 million, and after we look at his assets and liabilities, we trust that he can use 50% to 60% of his liquid assets for premiums."

FIGURE 14.3

For Premium Payments from Net Worth (calculated on net worth)	
Net Worth	$2,000,000+
Percentage of Net Worth Allowed for Total Planned Premium	Underwriter Discretion

If you're solidly affluent with over $2 million in net worth, the underwriter may decide to forgo the liquid asset evaluation and look instead at your overall financial picture. You might be selling properties, or have a business that is set to sell, so they may allow 20% or 30% of your net worth (not just the liquid assets) for for premiums (see Figure 14.3).

FIGURE 14.4

For Premium Payments from Windfall	
Percentage of Windfall Allowed for Total Planned Premium	Underwriter Discretion

Now what if you have a sudden lump sum come your way? The underwriter will gauge what percentage of that windfall can be used for your premiums (see Figure 14.4).

INSURANCE CAPACITY

Another qualifier, your demonstrated need, impacts the amount of death benefit you can receive, or your "insurance capacity." The insurance company calculates your maximum insurance capacity by using a formula that factors in things like your age and income or net worth. Often, the younger you are, the higher your insurance capacity. For example, when you're in your 30s, companies will typically qualify you for up to thirty times your income. So if you're earning $100,000 a year at age 32, if all other factors are favorable, you're likely going to qualify for as much as $3 million in insurance. As you age, the income multiplier decreases, which may also decrease your insurance capacity. In your 60s, it may be as low as five to ten times your income or a factor of your net worth.

The rationale behind insurance capacity is simple. When you're young and your family is heavily dependent on you for income and/or care, if you were to pass away, it would require a significant amount of money to make up for the loss of the income or care you would have provided. When you're older and your family is no longer as dependent on you, the need for the replacement of that income or net worth isn't as high. Whatever your insurance capacity is, if possible, it's often in your best interest to insure yourself to the maximum amount. But it's not imperative, and this is where you want to work closely with your IUL specialist to determine the right size premium bucket for you.

For example, let's say you are retired at age 60. You won't be demonstrating a need for income replacement, rather for estate preservation. The insurance company will project what your estate will be worth in the future, using an average of 5% to 8% growth, and factor in your age, as well. If you're age 40 or under, your insurance company will likely project twenty years of growth (fifteen years for ages 41 to 60, ten years for ages 61 to 70, and up to 75% of your life expectancy after age 70).

Let's say your estate has a net worth of $2 million, of which $1,250,000 is liquid. Using a growth rate of 8%, the insurance company will project

your estate to be worth over $5.8 million in fifteen years. The insurance company determines it can insure you for up to 55% of that net worth, for a death benefit of over $3.2 million. That requires a premium bucket of about $1 million.

Does that mean you'll automatically put in $1 million? No, for several reasons. First of all, the insurance company will also assess affordability guidelines. Since your premiums are coming from net worth, in this example, the insurance company will allow around 40% of your liquid net worth to go into the policy. Doing the math, 40% of $1,250,000 is $500,000.

So instead of trying to stretch (and possibly put yourself in financial harm's way) by using all $1 million of your insurance capacity, you are limited to a $500,000 Guideline Single Premium. This is wise, as it's right-sized for your situation.

OPTIONS FOR MAXIMIZING THAT CAPACITY

Now let's look at another option if you were in this situation, at age 60 with a net worth of $2 million, limited to a $500,000 premium bucket (due to affordability guidelines). What if you knew in a few years you were going to inherit a lump sum of $500,000 from your parents who are in their late 80s, and you'd like to put that additional half-million you anticipate getting into an IUL LASER Fund? But you know there's a chance that something could happen as you get older—an illness or heart problems—and you might not be able to qualify medically for another IUL LASER Fund.

You could pass your medical exam with flying colors today and open an inexpensive term policy. In a few years when you acquire that $500,000, you can convert your term policy into an IUL LASER Fund and maximum fund it over the next five years. Or, instead of a term policy, you could open an IUL LASER Fund designed to hold $500,000, and simply minimum fund it for the first four years or more, until you receive the inheritance. Once the windfall comes in, you can catch up the back premiums on your policy. For example, if your windfall comes in three years after you purchased your policy and you had paid $50,000 in premiums to keep your policy going, you could add another $250,000 to get to the $300,000 you are entitled to put in (without violating TAMRA rules). With either approach, it won't matter what your health is now, because the health status you received at age 60 will be grandfathered into your policy.

Whether you have $2 million in net worth with a half-million-dollar inheritance on the way, or you're age 35 with a young family and more modest means, this method can be a valuable, safe way to maximize your insurance capacity, especially if your liquid assets are currently more like a flowing stream than a raging river.

ADDING EVEN MORE TO YOUR IUL LASER FUND

If you recall, each IUL LASER Fund is structured with a Guideline Single Premium (GSP). According to TEFRA/DEFRA, that GSP is the maximum amount you can put into your policy during the funding phase. What if you get down the road, and you have more money you would like to set aside in an IUL LASER Fund? You can open another policy, or you can take advantage of what we call the 1/11th Rule. According to TEFRA/DE-FRA, starting in Years 11 to 15, depending on your age, you can add more money to your policy each year: up to the Guideline Level Premium.

To illustrate, let's say your IUL LASER Fund has a GSP of $500,000. You maximum funded your policy within the first five years. Now, let's say starting in Year 12, you wanted to add up to the Guideline Level Premium (sometimes called the Guideline Annual Premium) each year for the rest of your life. Adding up to the Guideline Level Premium does not require you to buy any more insurance. It is simply a powerful way to set aside additional money in a safe, tax-favored environment, with predictable rates of return, liquidity, and of course, income-tax-free death benefit that passes on to your heirs. This option is ideal for people who may have encountered health challenges after opening their initial IUL LASER Fund, challenges that prevent them from opening another policy.

DIVERSITY WITHIN YOUR IUL LASER FUND

As you look at your IUL LASER Fund, you can apply a diversified approach to how you put the money in your policy to work. We're talking about your index strategies—you can choose more than one index, and you can change the indexes you use from year-to-year (or every two or five years, depending on your index segment term).

For example, if we take a look at one of our client's policies, a recent snapshot shows the latest annual growth on her maximum-funded

IUL policy. She has chosen four different index strategies for her policy. During this last year, one of those strategies performed at 5%, one at 8%, one at 10%, and one at 15%.

You may look at this and think, "Too bad she didn't just put it all in the index strategy that saw a 15% return!" And that may have been true for this particular year. But because markets are prone to ups and downs, twists and turns, it may be wise to spread the risk out among different indexes, as each may be impacted differently by the market's whims. Many of our clients choose similar diversified strategies, taking advantage of the safety in having their money at work in different indexes.

Keep in mind you can also change up your index strategies at the end of each index segment term. This is one of the many good reasons to connect with your IUL specialist on an annual basis, to assess how your policy indexing performed in the previous year and make any adjustments you feel appropriate for the coming year.

What about diversification among IUL LASER Funds? As we've mentioned, after opening and funding your initial maximum-funded IUL policy, if you come upon additional money to set aside for your future, you can open another IUL LASER Fund ... and another ... and so on. When doing so, you may want to consider doing what we do—opening policies with the different reputable companies we recommend. This way you're benefiting from the variations in the features offered by these insurance companies.

A FOUNDATION FOR SUCCESS

Diversification within your IUL LASER Fund isn't our only recommendation. We generally recommend putting as much as you can into an IUL LASER Fund (up to your maximum affordability guideline percentage, typically 20% to 40% of your income or net worth, if possible). And the rest?

We recommend utilizing a blend of strategies, and we believe it is your right—and responsibility—to be critical in assessing which vehicles deserve your attention, and your money. As mentioned in Section I, Chapter 4, because we use liquidity, safety, rate of return, and tax advantages to analyze financial vehicles, we have developed a proprietary LASER

Rating System™ to create comparisons based on how well financial vehicles deliver on these four elements, using a 1 to 10 scale (with 10 being the top score).

We have found some vehicles may score well in some areas, low in others—all products have give and take. For example, take a traditional savings account—it typically scores high in liquidity and safety, but lower in rate of return and tax advantages. A typical 401(k) invested in the market scores moderately in rate of return and tax advantages, but can be lower in liquidity and safety.

The IUL LASER Fund scores well in all four categories as compared to other financial vehicles, which is essentially why we call this type of maximum-funded, properly structured IUL policy: The IUL LASER Fund. (Note: The LASER Ratings in Figures 14.5 and 14.6 are based on a fully-funded insurance contract. An insurance contract that is not fully-funded would have lower ratings.)

FIGURE 14.5

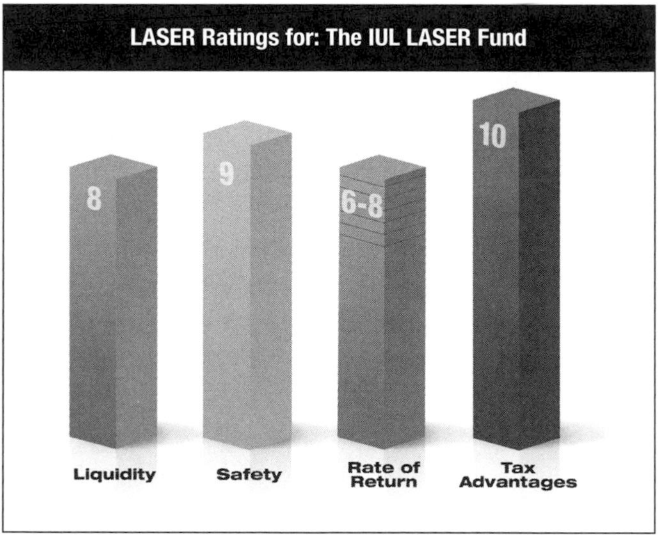

LASER Ratings for: The IUL LASER Fund

Liquidity 8 Safety 9 Rate of Return 6-8 Tax Advantages 10

FIGURE 14.6

	RATING	DETAILS
LIQUIDITY	8	You can access cash value by contacting the insurance company. Funds are generally available in 3-10 days. No government penalties exist for accessing your reserves. Most often, you'll want to access your cash value through a loan provision (loans are specifically designed to comply with IRS guidelines for tax-free access). In early years, accessing cash value may hurt long-term policy performance.
SAFETY	9	– Safety of Principal: Cash value is not subject to market volatility and is protected from market risk. Products have a 0% floor during down markets. If you do not properly fund your policy, long-term performance may suffer due to policy fees and expenses. – Safety of Institution: Monies are held in an insurance company portfolio. The insurance industry is highly regulated to protect policy holders.
RATE OF RETURN	6-8	Rates of return can be either fixed interest, indexed interest, or a combination of both. Rates can be tied to market-based potential growth through indexing. Products we recommend generally have indexed returns that have historically averaged from 5% to 10%.
TAX ADVANTAGES	10	Money grows tax-deferred. Most often, you'll access your cash value tax-free through loans. Upon your death, your death benefit transfers income-tax-free to your beneficiaries. Any policy loans from the accumulation value are income tax-free while the policy remains in force. Surrendering your policy may cause a taxable event. Seek professional tax advice for your specific situation.

The IUL LASER Fund ranks higher overall than other financial vehicles in our opinion, but other strategies have their "LASER merits," and their place in a well-rounded financial portfolio.

As you explore other financial vehicles to construct your financial future, keep the LASER Rating in mind. Work with your financial professional to identify vehicles that can help you move toward abundance with as much liquidity, safety, rate of return, and tax advantages as possible.

The key here is when you have a good portion of your money in an IUL LASER Fund, benefiting from its liquidity, safety, predictable rates of return, and tax advantages, you have a solid foundation on which you can build the rest of your financial strategies. With the strength of a properly structured, maximum-funded IUL policy as your base, you can afford to complement your portfolio with traditional vehicles with fairly solid LASER Ratings, such as 401(k)s and IRAs, Fixed Indexed Annuities, Assets Under Management, and more. Let's take a moment here to examine some of those options.

WHAT ABOUT MONEY ALREADY IN TRADITIONAL VEHICLES?

We have many clients who come to us with significant amounts of money already in traditional financial vehicles, such as IRAs and 401(k)s. As we mentioned earlier in the book, IRAs and 401(k)s have their limitations (especially when you get hit with taxes as you withdraw your money during retirement). That said, they can still provide value to your financial portfolio—especially if your employer offers contribution matching. And because we believe in a balanced approach, there's no need for alarm about these accounts' less than stellar marks on the LASER Test.

Depending on your situation, it may be better to leave your money right where it is, or you may want to take advantage of other options, such as "going to cash," exploring strategic rollouts, or rolling the qualified funds over into financial vehicles that give you guaranteed income, with market protection, all while earning market rates of return.

For example, say you have $500,000 in a 401(k), and you're age 60. The market starts to take a nosedive, like it did in 2008. Your fee-based advisor can help you "go to cash" with all or part of the money in your account. This way your money is still in the 401(k), benefiting from the tax-deferred treatment, but now it is purely cash. It is no longer invested in mutual funds, stocks, or indexes that can drag down your account value as the market tanks. When the market picks up again, you can choose to put your money back into the market in a managed money environment, or perform a strategic rollout.

With strategic rollouts, you can systematically transition your money from your IRA or 401(k) to an IUL LASER Fund. Essentially, the objectives of a strategic rollout are to: 1) get your taxes over and done with, and 2) reposition money in an IUL LASER Fund so you can benefit from greater liquidity, safety, predictable rates of return, tax-free income during retirement, and an income-tax-free death benefit for your heirs.

Going back to paying taxes on the seed rather than the harvest, the challenge with IRAs and 401(k)s is that you're required to do the opposite. With these accounts, you pay tax on the harvest rather than the seed, because that arrangement benefits Uncle Sam—often at your expense.

To avoid unnecessary taxes during retirement, it can make financial sense to move money from IRAs and 401(k)s to an IUL LASER Fund. If

done correctly, it's possible to stay within your same tax bracket and even offset some or all of the tax incurred during the rollout by resurrecting certain tax deductions. It's also possible to move a greater volume of money out during tax-advantaged years (whether that's because of current tax laws or personal income situations). In Section II, we'll examine real-life examples of how strategic rollouts can open the way for more abundance.

ANNUITIES

Financial vehicles that provide guaranteed income can ensure vital peace of mind during retirement. Annuities can be used to provide predictable income streams during retirement, in addition to Social Security (which may change in the future) and pensions.

With that in mind, annuities can be an ideal complement to your financial portfolio, keeping in mind they are a long-term financial vehicle used primarily for retirement income. Now not all annuities are created equal. There are some annuities we steer clients away from. With the variable annuity, for example, you are assuming the risk, not the insurance company, because your money is directly in the market (typically in mutual funds and/or stocks of your choice). So if the market tanks, so does your annuity. Not so safe, right? That's why this type of annuity is not high on our list.

The primary annuity we recommend is a Fixed Indexed Annuity, because it has similar indexing features as a properly structured IUL. Let's take a moment to look at the FIA through the LASER lens. (See Figures 14.7 and 14.8)

FIGURE 14.7

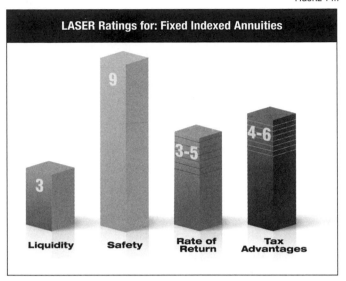

LASER Ratings for: Fixed Indexed Annuities

| | | | |
| Liquidity | Safety | Rate of Return | Tax Advantages |

FIGURE 14.8

	RATING	DETAILS
LIQUIDITY	3	Liquid up to 10% with no surrender charge on most products. Liquidity can differ based on the annuity you select. (Taxes may be due upon distribution.)
SAFETY	9	- Safety of Principal: Assets in a Fixed Indexed Annuity are not subject to market volatility. - Guaranteed Income: When you're ready to turn on income, amounts can be guaranteed for life. - Safety of Institution: Monies are held in an insurance company portfolio. The insurance industry is highly regulated to protect policyholders. We suggest A.M. Best rated A+ Superior companies.
RATE OF RETURN	3-5	Rates of return can either be fixed interest, indexed interest, or a combination of both. Rates can be tied to market-based potential growth through indexing. Rates are generally lower due to guaranteed income and payout options.
TAX ADVANTAGES	4-6	Money grows tax-deferred. Distributions are subject to ordinary income tax and, if taken before age 59½, a 10% federal additional tax may apply. Seek professional tax advice for your specific situation.

As you can see in Figure 14.8, liquidity is not as high as with a properly structured IUL. And unlike an IUL LASER Fund, you can't borrow from your FIA income-tax-free. If you want to access money from your FIA, you will pay taxes on the gains (unless your FIA is a Roth IRA FIA).

As for safety advantages, FIAs are incredible and on par with an IUL LASER Fund. You're protected by a guaranteed floor during down years, and during up years, your gains are locked in, and your FIA resets.

When it comes to predictable rates of return and index strategies, FIAs have similar benefits to IUL LASER Funds, just on a smaller scale. With an FIA, you'll see lower caps and participation rates. However, many FIAs come with no fees (which can help offset the lower returns), or a 1% fee (usually associated with a guaranteed income feature or rider).

Looking at tax advantages, like IUL LASER Funds, FIAs enjoy tax-deferred growth. However, unlike an IUL LASER Fund, you will pay taxes on those gains when you withdraw money from your FIA.

For their strengths in safety and tax advantages, FIAs can be a strong component of your comprehensive financial plan.

MORE ON AT-RETIREMENT PLANNING

As you can see, for a well-rounded financial future, you want a well-rounded financial portfolio. That balance will help you not only address your various financial needs, but you'll also enjoy greater safety and peace of mind with a comprehensive approach.

Throughout most of this book, we've focused on optimal ways to save **for retirement** (and other long-term financial goals), using financial vehicles that ideally provide a combination of liquidity, safety, rate of return, and tax advantages throughout the four phases of retirement planning.

Now we want to delve a little deeper into a concept we introduced in Section I, Chapter 2: **at-retirement** planning. This focuses on the types of financial vehicles that can generate optimal net-spendable income during retirement. Figure 14.9 illustrates the four different categories of income that you can customize for your own portfolio. Your approach to retirement could include one, two, or even all of the categories below:

FIGURE 14.9

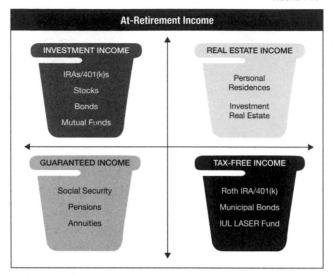

Let's highlight some of the common financial vehicles that fall under these four categories.

Investment Income – 0% to 50%

Investment income usually results from investments in the market like stocks, mutual funds, and bonds. Many or most IRAs or 401(k)s are invested in the market. (The unfortunate thing is most Americans have 80% to 90% in this category, which we feel is top-heavy). Investment income can score high on liquidity and rate of return, but usually scores low on safety. We recommend 0% to 50% of your retirement income should come from this category.

Real Estate Income – 0% to 40%

Real estate income typically comes from rental or lease income from real estate. Generally, real estate income can score well in tax advantages, but it often does not fare well in liquidity and safety. When it comes to rate of return, real estate income is often not optimized, depending on its location. We recommend 0% to 40% of your retirement income should come from this category.

Guaranteed Income - 10% to 80%

Guaranteed income can include Social Security benefits, pensions, and certain types of annuities. These kinds of vehicles score high in safety but very low in liquidity. They typically do not score well on rate of return, and there are little to no tax advantages. Depending on your objectives, we recommend 10% to 80% of your retirement income should come from this category.

Tax-Free Income - 30% to 60% (IUL LASER Fund)

Tax-free income can include municipal bonds, Roth IRAs/401(k)s, and of course IUL LASER Funds. Tax-free bond funds don't fare as well in rate of return as IUL LASER Funds, and most high-risk investments are not attractive to retirees because they score so low in safety. A properly structured and funded IUL LASER Fund can pass with the highest overall LASER Rating System™ score. Hence we recommend 30% to 60% of your retirement income should come from The IUL LASER Fund.

We help people diversify their retirement income to maintain a healthy balance among all four types of income. We also help clients optimize the allocation of that income to minimize taxes. For example, let's say you have $200,000 in annual retirement income in taxable income categories. You may want to reposition that money so that only $100,000 is coming from taxable income categories and $100,000 is coming from tax-free income categories. This way you're still enjoying $200,000 of annual cash flow income, but paying less in taxes.

By "re-categorizing" what type of income you're living on in retirement, in this example, you are saving yourself $27,000 in taxes (in a 27% tax bracket), thus increasing your net-spendable income by $27,000. (Otherwise, to achieve this same level of tax reduction, you would need to create a $100,000 tax deduction, such as a gift to a bonafide charity of $100,000—if you qualify to take this level of charitable deduction based on your adjusted gross income.)

As you can see, it's never too late to optimize your net-spendable income. While it's ideal to initiate a balanced, LASER-focused approach at the outset of your for-retirement planning phase, you can make adjustments at any point, even during the at-retirement phase, to improve your financial situation. If you recall, there's an adage that says, an

ounce of prevention is worth a pound of cure. If you're a young reader, this book serves as that ounce of prevention. If you're closer to retirement, this book can provide that pound of cure.

YOUR FUTURE, YOUR LEGACY

In essence, this book is all about your future, your legacy. Our aim is to provide you the knowledge you deserve to approach your future with clarity and confidence. As we look back over Section I, you can see we started with a discussion on creative destruction—how pivotal ideas come along and disturb the status quo to effect positive change.

As we reviewed the history of insurance, we saw the point in time when creative destruction initiated a seismic shift, with E.F. Hutton introducing Universal Life policies. We observed how things continued to evolve as pioneers in the industry championed the benefits of a properly structured, maximum-funded IUL policy for Americans, leading us to today, where people like you can be reading all about it in a book like this.

We also identified the elements of a prudent financial vehicle, exploring liquidity, safety, predictable rates of return, and tax advantages. We explored how The IUL LASER Fund provides all of these elements, and then some (with significant tax-free income and income-tax-free death benefit advantages, as well).

We've compared, poked, prodded, and examined The IUL LASER Fund from several analytical, left-brained angles. And now in Section II, we invite you to explore The IUL LASER Fund from a right-brained perspective. We'll share real-life examples of how actual clients of ours have utilized The IUL LASER Fund.

You'll be able to see an IUL LASER Fund can be more than a battery, powering your financial growth for a limited period of time. You'll explore how it can be a generator, fueling not only your Authentic Wealth, but also the abundance of your future generations.

So get ready to flip this book over and delve into stories that may just reflect your own someday. After all, it's *your* legacy you're building; congratulations on pursuing an abundant one!

TOP 5 TAKEAWAYS

1. As you look ahead to your financial future, you want to create a diverse **for-retirement** portfolio of financial strategies that provide balance.

2. You also want to choose strategies that provide the most liquidity, safety, predictable rates of return, and tax advantages possible—the LASER Rating System™ can help you compare different vehicles based on these features.

3. With its high LASER Ratings, The IUL LASER Fund provides a sound foundation for your financial future—and the opportunity to fuel a life of abundance in several ways, as we'll share in Section II. Other financial strategies, like Fixed Indexed Annuities, Assets Under Management, and others can play a valuable role in your **for-retirement** portfolio.

4. You also want to ensure you have a balanced **at-retirement** portfolio, which could include investment income, real estate income, guaranteed income, and tax-free income.

5. However you decide to approach your financial future, do so with a commitment to gaining knowledge and understanding. Take the time to empower yourself to make decisions that are best for your circumstances, and for an abundant future for you and your posterity.

Flip to Read Section II